Tensor Machine Learning: From Fundamental to Advanced Application

By

Jeffery M. Falgoust

Tensor machine learning

Tensor machine learning

Presentation of the book

In the quickly developing domain of AI and man-made consciousness, TensorFlow has arisen as a principal structure, driving development and preparing for momentous applications. Welcome to "TensorFlow Machine Learning: From Fundamental to Advanced Application." This book is your key to opening the unimaginable capability of AI, offering an excursion that begins with the rudiments and takes you to the outskirts of state-of-the-art applications.

AI has changed how we cooperate with innovation, from discourse acknowledgment in our cell phones to self-driving vehicles exploring our roads. With TensorFlow, an open-source AI library created by Google, you can jump profoundly into the core of this groundbreaking field. Our process starts with an extensive investigation of the principal ideas hidden in TensorFlow. We will unwind the complexities of information stream charts, tensors, tasks, and factors, giving you a solid groundwork in the centre rules that make TensorFlow so hearty and versatile. As we dive into active models and genuine applications, you'll find how to construct and prepare your own AI models, from straight relapse to complex brain organisations.

Be that as it may, this book isn't just about the fundamentals. We perceive that the genuine fervour in AI lies in its high-level applications, where you can use your insight to take care of mind-boggling issues. You'll investigate the domains of profound picking up, wandering into the universe of convolutional brain networks for picture examination, and intermittent brain networks for arrangement of information. You'll perceive the way moving learning and pre-prepared models can launch your tasks higher than ever.

Moreover, "TensorFlow Machine learning " is intended to give you experiences into state-of-the-art points and viable exhortation to assist you with exploring the intricacies of the field. Whether you are keen on normal language handling, support learning, or making your generative workmanship, this book will act as your dependable aide.

Chapter 1: The Machine learning landscape

AI isn't just about creating models; it's tied in with understanding how to successfully prepare and streamline them. We'll disentangle the secrets of misfortune capabilities, enhancement methods, and the craft of hyperparameter tuning. You'll likewise find the significance of regularisation and dropout to guarantee your models are strong and dependable.

As you progress, we'll direct you through the most common way of conveying your models to this present reality. You'll figure out how to commodity and serve your TensorFlow models, investigate TensorFlow Serving, and adjust models for versatile and edge gadgets with TensorFlow Light.

To genuinely get a handle on the force of AI, you want to observe it in real life. That is the reason we've included common sense applications, from picture order to time series gauging, permitting you to perceive how these methods are utilised in reality. We won't stop at essentially constructing and conveying models. Scaling and disseminated TensorFlow are likewise at the core of this book. You'll acquire a comprehension of how to appropriate your preparation across different machines and influence GPUs and TPUs to supercharge your tasks. Genuine contextual analyses exhibit the different utilizations of AI, from medical care and money to diversion and virtual entertainment. These models will move you and give understanding of how AI can upset different ventures. However, AI isn't without its moral contemplations. In the last sections, we'll address the significance of moral practices and capable man-made intelligence, guaranteeing that you approach your tasks with a sharp consciousness of the expected cultural effect.

As we set out on this excursion through "TensorFlow AI," we recollect that AI is a powerful field, continually developing. This book, established in TensorFlow 2. x, sets you up for the always-changing scene of artificial intelligence. We welcome you to investigate, learn, and develop, outfitted with the information and abilities to flourish in the astonishing universe of AI. We should start this excursion together, from basics to cutting-edge applications, and open the maximum capacity of TensorFlow.

The Machine Learning Landscape: Past, Present, and Future

AI, a subset of man-made reasoning (simulated intelligence), has arisen as one of the most extraordinary and quickly developing fields in the cutting edge mechanical scene. In this thorough investigation of the AI scene, we will travel through its authentic roots, grasp the center ideas, dive into its present-day applications, and companion into the astonishing future that lies ahead. From hypothetical establishments to functional ramifications, this 2000-word exposition plans to give an all-encompassing viewpoint on the AI scene.

Verifiable Roots and Foundations

To see the value in the AI scene, we should begin toward the start. The idea of machines that can learn and adjust their conduct traces back to the mid-twentieth 100 years. Momentous work by Alan Turing and others established the hypothetical starting points for AI. Turing's paper on "Processing Hardware and Insight" (1950) represented the popular Turing Test, a benchmark for machine knowledge that stays persuasive right up to the present day.

The improvement of electronic PCs during the twentieth century was a significant defining moment. With computational power available to them, analysts started to investigate the chance of making calculations that could mimic human learning. In 1956, the Dartmouth Studio, coordinated by John McCarthy, Marvin Minsky, Nathaniel Rochester, and Claude Shannon, denoted the introduction of computer-based intelligence as a field of exploration, which included AI as a central part.

Early AI calculations, for example, the perceptron, the antecedent to brain organisations, were created in the last part of the 1950s by Plain Rosenblatt. These calculations were restricted in their capacities, principally appropriate for directly divisible issues. By the way, they set up for additional investigation and improvement.

The Ascent and Fall of simulated intelligence: The man-made intelligence Winter

AI and simulated intelligence appreciated significant consideration and financing all through the 1960s and 1970s. Master frameworks, rule-based artificial intelligence, and representative thinking frameworks became well-known approaches. Notwithstanding, these early artificial intelligence frameworks confronted huge constraints, for example, their failure to deal with vulnerability and complex undertakings.

This prompted the first "Computer-based intelligence winter" during the 1970s, a period set apart by decreased interest and subsidising for computer-based intelligence and AI research. Assumptions had been set excessively high, and the field confronted moves it was not yet prepared to address. This respite endured through the 1980s.

Resurgence: The Introduction of Present-day Machine Learning

The 1990s saw the resurgence of AI, because of a conversion of elements. Propels in computational power, calculations, and the accessibility of enormous datasets reignited interest in the field. AI pioneers like Geoffrey Hinton, Yann LeCun, and Yoshua Bengio began to foster the groundwork of profound realisation, which would later change the field.

Furthermore, the web and advanced innovations produced tremendous measures of information, which became fundamental for preparing and testing AI calculations. This time denoted the progress from rule-based frameworks to information-driven approaches. Utilizations of AI began to build up forward momentum in different spaces, from money and medical services to normal language handling and PC vision.

The Information Unrest: Large Information and Machine Learning

The AI scene took a stupendous jump forward with the coming of huge information. Associations perceived the worth of information as an essential resource, and AI turned into a foundation for information examination and direction. The three Versus — Volume, Speed, and Assortment — characterised enormous information, and AI was instrumental in removing experiences from this downpour of data.

AI calculations were developed to deal with huge datasets and high-layered spaces. Methods like choice trees, support vector machines, and arbitrary woods tracked down their place close by brain organisations, offering assorted answers for various issue spaces.

The Profound Learning Revolution

The defining moment for AI accompanied the ascent of profound learning. Profound brain organisations, propelled by the construction and capability of the human cerebrum, exhibited striking abilities in dealing with complex errands. Convolutional Brain Organizations (CNNs) acquired forward leaps of PC vision, empowering machines to distinguish objects in pictures with shocking exactness. Repetitive Brain Organizations (RNNs) turned into the decision for consecutive information examination, for example, regular language handling and discourse acknowledgment.

The ImageNet Huge Scope Visual Acknowledgment Challenge (ILSVRC) rivalry in 2012 denoted a pivotal occasion. A profound learning model named AlexNet, created by Alex Krizhevsky, Ilya Sutskever, and Geoffrey Hinton, beat different methodologies overwhelmingly. This triumph flagged the appearance of profound advancement as the new worldview in AI.

The Brilliant Time: Applications and Impact

The effect of AI on society during the 21st century couldn't possibly be more significant. It has reshaped different ventures, making the inconceivable. Here are a few key spaces where AI has had a massive effect:

1. Healthcare: AI supports early sickness identification, clinical picture examination, and customised therapy suggestions.

2. Finance: Calculations foresee securities exchange patterns, distinguish false exchanges, and upgrade exchanging procedures.

3. Natural Language Handling (NLP): Chatbots, language interpretation, feeling examination, and voice acknowledgment have changed the manner in which we cooperate and interface with PCs.

4. Autonomous Vehicles: AI empowers self-driving vehicles to securely see and explore their current circumstance.

5. E-commerce: Recommender frameworks customise item suggestions for clients, further developing deals and consumer loyalty.

6. Entertainment: Content suggestion, gaming simulated intelligence, and content age have reformed media outlets.

7. Manufacturing: Prescient support and quality control frameworks have upgraded effectiveness and diminished margin time.

8. Environmental Science: AI breaks down environmental information, foresees cataclysmic events, and screens untamed life.

Challenges and Moral Concerns

The fast development of AI has delivered a few difficulties and moral worries. One of the first difficulties is the requirement for straightforwardness and interpretability. Profound learning models, while strong, frequently act as "secret elements," making it challenging to comprehend their choice-making processes. Predisposition in AI, originating from one-sided preparing information, is another basic concern. Models can propagate and try to enhance predispositions present in information, prompting crooked results in regions like law enforcement and employment. Information protection and security have additionally become principal. As AI frameworks depend on immense measures of information, guaranteeing the insurance of delicate data is pivotal.

Additionally, the social and monetary effects of computerization and simulated intelligence-driven work relocation require conscious thought. As machines progressively take on undertakings customarily performed by people, the requirement for reskilling and upskilling the labour force becomes clear.

Future Headings: AI Past 2020

The AI scene keeps on advancing, with a few invigorating patterns and future headings:

1. Explainable AI: Analysts are effectively chipping away at making simulated intelligence models more interpretable, permitting clients to comprehend how they show up at their choices.

2. Federated Learning: This approach empowers preparing on decentralised information sources, upgrading protection and security.

3. Quantum Machine Learning: Quantum registering vows to upset AI by taking care of complicated issues dramatically quicker.

4. AI for Healthcare: Advances in clinical imaging, drug revelation, and telemedicine are ready to change medical services.

5. AI in Edge Computing: Sending AI models to anxious gadgets like IoT sensors and cell phones will empower constant handling without depending on the cloud framework.

6. Ethical man-made intelligence Frameworks: Creating rules and guidelines for the moral utilisation of artificial intelligence and AI will be significant.

7. AI for Environment Change: AI can aid environment displaying, observing, and alleviation endeavours.

All in all, the AI scene has seen noteworthy development, from its hypothetical starting points to its viable applications in practically every area of the worldwide economy. As we keep on riding the influx of advancement, offsetting specialised progress with moral contemplations and mindful development is fundamental. AI can tackle a portion of humankind's most pressing difficulties, and with the right methodology, it can achieve positive, groundbreaking change.

What is TensorFlow?

TensorFlow is an open-source AI system created by the Google Cerebrum group. With its underlying delivery in 2015, TensorFlow has become one of the most well-known and broadly involved apparatuses for creating and sending AI models. In this 1000-word investigation, we will dive into what TensorFlow is, its key highlights, its applications, and its effect on the field of AI and man-made consciousness.

TensorFlow: A Presentation

TensorFlow gets its name from the centre activities it performs, which include the progression of information through tensors. Tensors are multi-faceted exhibits that can address shifting intricacy. These tensors are controlled through a computational diagram, where hubs address tasks and edges connote the progression of information between these tasks. The capacity to work with tensors in this chart-based worldview makes TensorFlow a strong and adaptable device for building AI models.

Key Elements of TensorFlow

1. Flexibility: TensorFlow is a flexible system that permits designers to fabricate an extensive variety of AI models, from basic straight relapse to complex profound brain organisations. Its adaptability makes it reasonable for different areas, including PC vision, regular language handling, and support learning.

2. Scalability: TensorFlow is intended to scale, from running on a solitary gadget to dispersed processing groups. This adaptability is critical for preparing enormous models on broad datasets, which is much of the time the case in cutting-edge research and modern applications.

3. Ease of Deployment: TensorFlow offers a few choices for model organisation, including TensorFlow Serving, TensorFlow Light, and TensorFlow.js. These apparatuses empower the consistent joining of AI models into creation frameworks, versatile applications, and web applications.

4. Community and Ecosystem: TensorFlow has an immense and dynamic local area of engineers, specialists, and professionals. This dynamic biological system has prompted the production of different significant-level APIs, libraries, and pre-prepared models, making it simpler to begin with AI and take care of genuine issues.

5. TensorBoard: TensorFlow accompanies a representation device called TensorBoard, which helps clients comprehend and investigate their models. It gives intelligent dashboards to investigate preparing measurements, model designs, and then some.

6. AutoML: TensorFlow gives AutoML devices that robotize a few parts of the AI cycle, for example, hyperparameter tuning and engineering search. These apparatuses, such as AutoKeras, assist clients with restricted AI aptitude in fabricating compelling models.

TensorFlow in real life

TensorFlow has made critical commitments to different fields, including PC vision, normal language handling, and support learning. Here are a few striking uses of TensorFlow:

1. Image Classification: Convolutional Brain Organizations (CNNs) worked with TensorFlow have accomplished momentous precision in picture order assignments. TensorFlow's undeniable level Programming interface, Keras, works on the advancement of CNN-based picture classifiers.

2. Object Detection: TensorFlow's article discovery models, like the Single Shot MultiBox Locator (SSD) and Quicker R-CNN, have been generally embraced for finding and distinguishing objects in pictures and video.

3. Natural Language Handling (NLP): In NLP, TensorFlow's Transformers models have set new principles in assignments like language interpretation, opinion examination, and text age. The BERT model, for instance, is a transformer-based design that has changed NLP.

4. Recommendation Systems: TensorFlow is utilized in building proposal frameworks, where it uses cooperative sifting and profound learning models to give customised suggestions to clients, as found in stages like Netflix and Amazon.

5. Speech Recognition: TensorFlow's discourse acknowledgment models have empowered progressions in voice associates and record administrations. It has been vital in making discourse-to-text and text-to-discourse frameworks.

6. Reinforcement Learning: TensorFlow is a famous decision for supporting learning undertakings, empowering the improvement of specialists who can figure out how to play computer games, control robots, and streamline complex frameworks.

7. Healthcare: TensorFlow is utilised in clinical imaging for errands like illness discovery and division. It supports the improvement of indicative instruments utilising profound learning models.

8. Finance: TensorFlow is utilised in monetary applications for misrepresentation discovery, risk evaluation, and stock cost expectation. Its flexibility permits it to adjust to a large number of monetary information examination undertakings.

TensorFlow's Effect

The effect of TensorFlow on the field of AI and computerised reasoning couldn't possibly be more significant. Here are a few manners by which it has impacted the space:

1. Accessibility: TensorFlow has democratised AI by giving open-source instruments and assets. It has brought the hindrance down to passage, empowering designers and scientists, everything being equal, to draw in with state-of-the-art man-made intelligence.

2. Research and Innovation: TensorFlow has been instrumental in cultivating advancement in the man-made intelligence field. Specialists can quickly model and examine novel models, prompting headways in profound learning designs and strategies.

3. Industry Adoption: Numerous enterprises have coordinated TensorFlow into their tasks. From medical care to back, organisations influence TensorFlow to upgrade independent direction, further develop client encounters, and robotize different cycles.

4. Education and Expertise Development: TensorFlow's accessibility and thorough documentation make it an important instrument for instructive purposes. It has empowered endless understudies and experts to acquire skills in AI.

5. State-of-the-Craftsmanship Models: TensorFlow is a typical stage for creating and sending cutting-edge AI models. This incorporates models for picture acknowledgment, regular language understanding, and support learning.

6. Open Source Collaboration: TensorFlow's open-source nature energises cooperation. Designers overall add to its turn of events, which results in a powerful and continually developing system.

Future Headings

Starting around my last information update in September 2021, TensorFlow was effectively advancing. The future bearings for TensorFlow may incorporate the accompanying:

1. Efficiency and Optimization: Persistent endeavours to enhance TensorFlow for both preparation and derivation are normal. This remembers upgrades for the equipment speed increase, model pressure, and quantization methods.

2. Explainability and Fairness: With the developing significance of morals and decency in artificial intelligence, TensorFlow may see upgrades in apparatuses and libraries for model logic and reasonableness assessment.

3. AutoML Advancement: TensorFlow's AutoML apparatuses may turn out to be significantly more available and refined, making it simpler for non-specialists to assemble top-notch models.

4. Edge and IoT: TensorFlow is probably going to assume a huge part in edge figuring and Web of Things (IoT) applications, permitting AI models to run on asset-compelled gadgets.

5. Hybrid Cloud and Dispersed Learning: With the rising utilisation of half-breed cloud conditions, TensorFlow may additionally grow its capacities for conveyed AI across cloud and on-premises foundations.

6. Interoperability: TensorFlow may keep on further developing interoperability with other AI and profound learning structures, taking into consideration smoother combinations with existing frameworks.

All in all, TensorFlow has been a main thrust in the headway of AI and man-made brainpower. Its adaptable, versatile, and open nature has enabled designers and scientists to make imaginative arrangements in different areas. Its people group-driven improvement and ceaseless development position it as an essential instrument for the simulated intelligence environment, with the potential for much more huge commitments in the years to come.

Setting up your environment

Setting up your environment climate is an essential initial step for working with devices like TensorFlow or some other programming errands. Beneath, I'll give general aid on setting up a Python-based climate for AI utilising TensorFlow. Kindly note that this is a significant level outline, and explicit advances can shift given your working framework and prerequisites.

1. Python Installation:

Guarantee that you have Python introduced to your framework. You can download Python from the authority site (https://www.python.org/downloads/) or utilise a dispersion like Boa Constrictor (https://www.anaconda.com/items/person) which incorporates numerous information science libraries.

2. Virtual Climate (Discretionary however Recommended):

Tensor machine learning

It's a decent practice to establish a virtual climate for your AI projects. This secludes your task's conditions from framework-wide Python bundles. You can establish a virtual climate utilising the 'venv' module or use Boa constrictor conditions on the off chance that you're utilising Boa constrictor.

For instance, to establish a virtual climate with 'venv':

```bash
python - m venv myenv
```

Activate the virtual environment:

- On Windows: 'myenv\Scripts\activate'

- On macOS and Linux: 'source myenv/bin/activate'

3. Installing TensorFlow:

With your virtual climate enacted, you can introduce TensorFlow utilising pip:

```bash
pip install tensorflow
```

You can introduce the computer chip just by rendering it with this order. On the off chance that you have a viable GPU, you can introduce the GPU rendition, which will use the GPU for quicker preparation. To introduce the GPU rendition, use:

```bash
pip install tensorflow-gpu
```

4. Incorporated Improvement Climate (IDE):

Pick an IDE for coding. A few well-known decisions for AI are Jupyter Scratchpad (which accompanies Boa constrictor) and incorporated improvement conditions like PyCharm, Visual Studio Code, or Spyder.

5. Extra Libraries:

Contingent upon your particular venture, you might require other Python libraries. For information control and examination, consider libraries like NumPy and Pandas. For perception, Matplotlib and Seaborn are normal decisions. You could likewise require sci-kit-learn for AI errands.

Introduce extra libraries utilising pip. For instance:

'''bash

pip install numpy pandas matplotlib sci-kit-learn

'''

6. Data:

Assemble or make the dataset you intend to work with. TensorFlow offers datasets employing the TensorFlow Datasets (TFDS) library. You can likewise import information from records utilising libraries like Pandas or NumPy.

7. Code Supervisor Setup:

Assuming you're utilising an IDE like PyCharm, Visual Studio Code, or Jupyter Journal, make a point to design your inclinations, expansions, and settings to suit your work process.

8. Composing and Running Code:

Begin composing your AI code. You can make models utilising TensorFlow and train them on your information. Make certain to allude to the authority TensorFlow documentation (https://www.tensorflow.org/) for direction on unambiguous undertakings and strategies.

9. Model Training:

While preparing your model, try to determine the fitting gadget (computer chip or GPU) assuming you introduced TensorFlow with GPU support. TensorFlow ought to naturally recognize and utilise accessible GPUs.

10. TensorBoard Integration:

Consider utilising TensorBoard, TensorFlow's representation apparatus, to screen and investigate your model's presentation. You can send it from the order line or automatically inside your code.

11. Saving Models:

In the wake of preparing your model, save it for some time in the future. TensorFlow gives instruments to save and load models.

12. Testing and Evaluation:

Assess your model's presentation on a test dataset and calibrate it depending on the situation.

13. Deployment:

If you intend to convey your model in a creative climate, examine TensorFlow Serving or TensorFlow Light for portable and edge arrangements. TensorFlow likewise gives change apparatuses to enhance your models for arrangement.

Setting up your current circumstance can be a point-by-point process, yet it's fundamental for useful and productive AI and profound learning work. Try to counsel the authority documentation of the devices and libraries you are utilising for a more unambiguous direction.

Chapter 2: Fundamentals of Tensorflow

TensorFlow is a strong and flexible open-source AI structure created by Google. To comprehend the essentials of TensorFlow, we should investigate the critical ideas and parts:

1. Tensors:

- The key information structure in TensorFlow is a tensor, which is a multi-faceted cluster. Tensors can address different information types, including scalars, vectors, frameworks, and higher-layered exhibits.

- Tensors are at the centre of TensorFlow's calculation and are passed between tasks in a computational chart.

2. Computational Graph:

- TensorFlow proposes a computational diagram to characterise and execute AI models. The diagram is a progression of interconnected hubs, where every hub addresses an activity.

- Tensors move through the chart, and activities are performed on them. This diagram-based approach takes into consideration dispersed figuring and improvement.

3. Operations (Ops):

- Tasks in TensorFlow are hubs in the computational chart. These tasks perform different calculations on tensors.

- Instances of tasks incorporate expansion, network duplication, and actuation capabilities, and that's just the beginning. TensorFlow gives a large number of inherent tasks.

4. Sessions:

- To execute tasks in TensorFlow, you want to make a meeting. A meeting embodies the condition of the TensorFlow runtime and runs the computational diagram.

- In TensorFlow 2. x, enthusiastic execution is the default, and that implies you can execute tasks without unequivocally making a meeting. Be that as it may, you can in any case involve meetings for similarity with TensorFlow 1. x and for some high-level use cases.

5. Variables:

- TensorFlow factors are utilised to keep up with the state across various calls to a capability. They are frequently utilised for model boundaries that should be refreshed during preparation.

- Factors should be expressly instated and can be refreshed utilising angle plummet or other enhancement methods.

6. Placeholders and Tensors:

- Placeholders are utilised to take care of information in the computational diagram. They resemble sections focused on information.

- Tensors, then again, can be utilised to store information and halfway outcomes inside the diagram.

7. Keras API:

- TensorFlow gives an undeniable level Programming interface called Keras that improves on the most common way of building and preparing profound learning models.

- Keras is incorporated into TensorFlow (from TensorFlow 2. x) and offers an easy-to-use and measured method for characterising brain organisations.

8. Layers and Models:

- In TensorFlow and Keras, you can make models by stacking layers. Layers are the structural blocks of brain organisation.

- Normal layers incorporate thick (completely associated) layers, convolutional layers, and repetitive layers.

9. Loss Functions:

- Misfortune capabilities evaluate how well a model is performing. In AI, the objective is frequently to limit misfortune.

- TensorFlow gives different inherent misfortune capabilities reasonable for various undertakings like mean squared blunder for relapse and straight-out cross-entropy for arrangement.

10. Optimizers:

- Analyzers are calculations used to change the model's boundaries during preparation to limit the misfortune capability.

- Normal enhancers incorporate stochastic angle drop (SGD), Adam, and RMSprop.

11. Callbacks:

- Callbacks are utilised in preparing to perform activities at explicit focus during preparation, like saving the model, early halting, or logging progress.

- TensorFlow/Keras gives callback components to different use cases.

12. Model Training:

- To prepare an AI or profound learning model, you commonly give preparing information, indicate a misfortune capability, an enhancer, and the quantity of preparing steps (ages).

- The model iteratively changes its boundaries to limit the misfortune by backpropagating inclinations.

13. Evaluation and Prediction:

- After preparing, you can assess your model's exhibition on a different dataset and make expectations on new information.

- TensorFlow gives capabilities to play out these errands.

14. Deployment:

- TensorFlow offers different ways of conveying prepared models for creation use. This can include TensorFlow Serving for serving models over the organisation, TensorFlow Light for versatile and inserted gadgets, and TensorFlow.js for web applications.

15. Community and Ecosystem:

- TensorFlow has a huge and dynamic local area of engineers and specialists. This has prompted the improvement of broad assets, libraries, and pre-prepared models for a great many applications.

16. TensorFlow Hub:

- TensorFlow Center point is a vault of pre-prepared models and model parts. It permits you to reuse and calibrate models for different undertakings without any problem.

17. TensorBoard:

- TensorBoard is an amazing asset for picturing and examining the preparation cycle and model execution. It helps in troubleshooting, observing, and upgrading your AI projects.

Understanding these basic ideas is vital for actually utilising TensorFlow to fabricate and send AI and profound learning models. TensorFlow's adaptability and versatility make it a well-known decision for a large number of utilizations across various spaces.

Tensorflow Data flow graphs

TensorFlow proposes information stream charts to address and execute calculations. Understanding information stream diagrams is fundamental for working with TensorFlow successfully. Here are the key ideas connected with information stream diagrams in TensorFlow:

1. Nodes (Activities or Ops):

- Hubs in a TensorFlow information stream chart address tasks, which are units of calculation. These activities can be numerical tasks, information changes, or variable tasks, from there, the sky's the limit.

- Every hub can take at least zero info tensors and produce at least one result tensor.

2. Edges (Tensor Values):

- Edges in the chart address the progression of information between hubs. They associate the result of one activity with the contribution of another.

- These edges convey tensor qualities, which are complex exhibits (scalars, vectors, grids, and so forth) that are worked on by the hubs.

3. Tensors:

- Tensors are the key information units in TensorFlow. They course through the edges of the information stream diagram.

- Tensors are permanent; when made, their qualities can't be changed. All things being equal, tasks make new tensors as a result.

4. Computational Graph:

- The information stream diagram is otherwise called the computational chart. It is a coordinated non-cyclic diagram (DAG) where hubs address tasks and edges address information streams.

- The construction of the chart characterises the arrangement of tasks and conditions.

5. Session:

- To execute tasks inside the diagram, you want to make a meeting. A meeting typifies the runtime climate for TensorFlow.

- During a meeting, the chart's hubs are assessed, and calculations are performed to create results.

6. Lazy Evaluation:

- TensorFlow follows a "sluggish assessment" approach. This means that, as a matter of course, the tasks are not executed quickly when characterised. All things being equal, they are added to the computational diagram for later execution.

- Sluggish assessment permits TensorFlow to productively enhance and perform tasks more.

7. Placeholders:

- Placeholders are hubs in the chart where you can take care of outside information in the diagram. They act as section focuses for information, particularly in situations where you need to enter information.

- Placeholders are regularly utilised for preparing information, approval information, and test information in AI models.

8. Variables:

- Factors are a unique kind of hub utilised for keeping up with the state across various calls to a capability or inside a model. They are frequently used to address model boundaries.

- Factors should be expressly instated and can be refreshed during preparation.

9. Control Dependencies:

- Now and again, you might need to indicate that specific tasks should be finished before others. This is finished utilising control conditions. You can authorise the request for execution in the chart.

10. Name Scopes:

- Name extensions are utilised for putting together hubs inside the chart. They permit you to gather related tasks for better lucidity and association.

11. Global Default Graph:

- TensorFlow keeps a worldwide default diagram, and tasks made without a trace of an expressly indicated chart are added to this default diagram.

- You can make your named charts assuming you want various autonomous diagrams in a similar program.

12. Importing and Trading Graphs:

- TensorFlow gives instruments for saving and reestablishing computational charts, which is fundamental for model industriousness and adaptability.

In synopsis, TensorFlow's information stream charts are an essential idea that underlies the whole TensorFlow structure. They characterise the calculations to be played out, the request in which they are executed, and the progression of information between activities. Understanding how to develop, assess, and improve information stream charts is fundamental for really utilising TensorFlow to assemble and prepare AI and profound learning models.

Tensors and Tasks in Profound Learning

In the domain of AI and profound picking up, understanding the centre ideas is fundamental. Among these primary ideas, tensors and tasks stand apart as the structure blocks whereupon the greater part of the field's calculations and models are built. In this broad investigation, we will dig into the complexities of tensors, their importance in profound learning, and the wide exhibit of tasks that can be performed on them.

What are Tensors?

The Pith of Tensors

At its centre, a tensor is a multi-layered exhibit that can address a tremendous scope of information. While this might sound dynamic, the idea of tensors is shockingly instinctive. Tensors can be considered speculations of scalars, vectors, and lattices. These numerical items act as the major information structure for putting away and controlling information in different aspects.

Scalar, Vector, Framework, Tensor

How about we separate the movement from scalars to tensors:

1. Scalar (0D Tensor): A scalar is a solitary number, similar to the number "42." With regards to tensors, we look at this as a 0D tensor.

2. Vector (1D Tensor): Moving one step up, we have vectors, which are 1D exhibits. For example, a rundown of whole numbers like '[1, 2, 3]' is a 1D tensor.

3. Matrix (2D Tensor): A grid is a 2D cluster, comprising lines and sections. Grids are frequently used to address information like pictures or plain information.

4. Higher-Layered Tensors: In past frameworks, tensors can have multiple aspects. A 3D tensor could address a variety of pictures with RGB channels, and a 4D tensor can address a succession of pictures.

In profound learning, higher-layered tensors become especially important. They are equipped for embodying complex information designs, and profound brain networks regularly work on these multifaceted tensors.

Meaning of Tensors in Profound Learning

Information Portrayal

Tensors are the go-to decision for addressing information in profound learning given their adaptability. Brain networks manage a heap of information types, like pictures, text, and sound. These information types can be effectively addressed as tensors. For example, an RGB picture can be put away as a 3D tensor, where each aspect relates to the level, width, and variety of channels.

Brain Organization Layers

Profound learning models, particularly brain organisations, are built as a progression of layers. These layers perform procedures on tensors. At the point when you feed information into a brain organisation, it goes through changes, frequently through procedures on tensors. Convolutional layers, completely associated layers, repetitive layers — each of these relies upon tensors as info and result.

Slope Plummet

In preparing profound learning models, enhancement calculations like slope plummet assume a focal part. These calculations include the estimation of slopes, which are subsidiaries of the model's boundaries. Angles are figured by backpropagating blunders through the organisation. This backpropagation is made effective through the control of tensors and the utilisation of procedures on them.

Tensor and operation

Now that we've laid out the significance of tensors in profound learning, how about we investigate the wide cluster of activities that can be performed on tensors?

1. Component Wise Activities

Component-wise tasks include applying an activity (e.g., expansion, increase, or a numerical capability) to every component of a tensor exclusively. These activities are critical for undertakings like standardisation and enactment capabilities. Normal models incorporate ReLU (Redressed Straight Unit) and the sigmoid capability. Component-wise activities can be performed on tensors of any aspect.

2. Network Increase

Network duplication is a crucial activity in direct variable-based maths, and it assumes a significant part in profound learning. In brain organisations, lattice duplication is utilised for direct changes, frequently executed in completely associated layers. At the point when you need to register weighted amounts of data sources, lattice duplication is the key. It likewise works with the progression of data between layers.

3. Reshaping

Reshaping permits you to change the shape or aspects of a tensor. Planning information for explicit layers in a brain network is frequently utilised. For instance, you could level a 2D tensor (e.g., a picture) into a 1D tensor to enter it into a completely associated layer. Reshaping tasks help in squeezing tensors into the necessary info states of various layers.

4. Interpretation

Translating a tensor includes trading its lines and sections. This activity is fundamental in lattice duplication, particularly while managing complex information. It empowers you to adjust the aspects of the duplication activity accurately. Practically speaking, it is habitually utilised in brain network executions.

5. Decrease Activities

Decreasing tasks plan to diminish the components of a tensor, normally by performing tasks like summation, averaging, or tracking down the most extreme or least qualities along unambiguous aspects. These tasks help in getting rundown measurements or accumulating data from tensors. For example, normal pooling in convolutional brain networks diminishes the spatial components of element maps while holding fundamental data.

6. Broadcasting

Broadcasting is an influential idea that permits tensors of various shapes to be consolidated in tasks. Fundamentally, more modest tensors are "broadcast" to match the state of bigger tensors, empowering component-wise activities. Broadcasting improves on numerous tasks, for example, adding a scalar to a tensor or joining tensors with various yet viable shapes.

7. Link and Parting

The link includes consolidating tensors along unambiguous aspects. This is valuable when you need to blend information from various sources or layers. On the other hand, parting permits you to partition a tensor into more modest parts along a picked aspect. These activities are significant while planning brain networks with complex structures, like Siamese organisations or multi-branch models.

8. Convolution

Convolution is a particular activity utilised fundamentally in convolutional brain organisations (CNNs). It includes applying a channel (otherwise called a bit) to an information tensor, which is especially compelling for handling multi-layered information like pictures. Convolution empowers highlights to be removed proficiently from input information, making it an essential activity for picture handling and PC vision undertakings.

Uses of Tensors and Tasks

The flexibility of tensors and their related tasks permits them to be utilised in an extensive variety of profound learning applications:

1. Picture Characterization

In picture characterization undertakings, convolutional brain organisations (CNNs) are generally utilised. Tensors and convolution tasks are essential to CNNs, empowering organisations to learn and perceive multifaceted examples in pictures.

2. Regular Language Handling

In regular language handling (NLP), repetitive brain organisations (RNNs), transformers, and different models depend on tensors to handle text information. Tensors address the embeddings of words or subword units, and different procedures on these tensors permit models to comprehend and create human language.

3. Support Learning

Support learning calculations, which are applied to errands like game-playing specialists and mechanical technology, additionally rely upon tensors. The state, activity, and prize information are frequently addressed as tensors, and the procedure on these tensors guides the specialist's dynamic interaction.

4. Object Discovery and Division

PC vision undertakings, like item identification and picture division, influence tensors and convolutional tasks broadly. These tasks assist in recognizing and portraying objects in pictures, empowering applications with liking independent vehicles and clinical picture examination.

5. Generative Models

Generative models like Generative Ill-disposed Organisations (GANs) make new satisfaction by gaining from existing information. Tensors assume a basic part in these models, where tasks create engineered information that intently looks like the preparation information. GANs, specifically, have been utilised for creating pictures, text, and even music.

In conclusion, Tensors and tasks are the foundation of profound picking up, supporting information portrayal, brain network layers, and advancement strategies. Tensors, going from scalars to higher-layered exhibits, give the resources to productively address and control information. The large number of activities that can be applied to tensors empower complex calculations and changes, making profound learning models versatile to different errands and information types.

Variables and placeholders

Understanding tensors and their tasks is pivotal for anybody diving into the field of AI and man-made reasoning. The transaction between these key ideas frames the establishment whereupon progressed models and applications are assembled. As the field of profound learning keeps on advancing, so does the significance of dominating tensors and their tasks in driving development and tackling complex issues.

Tensor machine learning

With regards to AI, factors, and placeholders are major ideas frequently connected with the TensorFlow library. These ideas assume an urgent part in characterising and executing computational diagrams for preparing and deriving profound learning models.

Definition

Factors in TensorFlow are utilised to hold and refresh model boundaries during preparation. They address tensors whose values can be changed. Factors are normally utilised to store loads and predispositions in brain organisations, and they assume a key part in the growing experience.

Key Qualities

1. Mutable State: Dissimilar to constants or placeholders (which we'll talk about straightaway), factors have alterable states. This implies their qualities can be refreshed as the model gains from the preparation information.

2. Initialization: Factors should be initiated with introductory qualities before they are utilised. Normal introduction strategies incorporate arbitrary statements or stacking pre-prepared loads.

3. Gradient Computation: Factors are important for the computational diagram for angle calculation during backpropagation. This implies their inclinations can be processed and used to refresh their qualities through improvement calculations like slope plunge.

Model Utilisation

This is an illustration of the way factors are ordinarily utilised in TensorFlow to characterise loads and predispositions in a basic brain or values are given at runtime.

2. Shape Specification: Placeholders require a shape to be indicated when they are made. This is frequently used to characterise the normal state of info information.

network:

'''python

import tensorflow as tf

Define weights and biases as variables weights= tf.Variable(tf.random.normal([input_dim, output_dim]), name='weights')

Biases = tf.Variable(tf.zeros([output_dim]), name='biases')

'''

In the code above, 'loads' and 'predispositions' are characterised as factors with irregular beginning qualities. During preparation, these factors will be refreshed to limit the misfortune.

Placeholders

Placeholders are utilised to take care of information in a TensorFlow computational diagram. They go about as the section focuses on information that will be given when the chart is executed. Placeholders are especially valuable while building the info pipeline for preparing, where you could have various clumps of preparing information.

Key Attributes

1. Immutable: Not at all like factors, placeholders are unchanging; you can't change their qualities whenever they are characterised.

Model Utilisation

This is an illustration of the way placeholders can be utilised to characterise input information for a computational diagram:

'''python

import tensorflow as tf

Define a placeholder for input data

input_data = tf.placeholder(tf.float32, shape=(None, input_dim))

Characterise an activity that utilises the placeholder

yield = some_operation(input_data)

'''

In the code above, 'input_data' is a placeholder that expects information of shape '(None, input_dim)'. During diagram execution, you would take care of real information in this placeholder.

When to Utilise Factors and Placeholders

Factors and placeholders fill various needs:

- Use **variables** to store and refresh model boundaries that should be picked up during preparation, like loads and predispositions in a brain organisation.

- Use **placeholders** to characterise the contributions to your model, which you'll give real information at runtime. Placeholders are regularly utilised for input information, names, or whatever other information that isn't advanced by the model.

In present-day TensorFlow renditions (2. x and later), factors are frequently less ordinarily utilised contrasted with before adaptations, on account of the presentation of significant level APIs like Keras, which handles variable administration and preparing circle subtleties for you. Notwithstanding, understanding the basic ideas of factors and placeholders is as yet significant for further developed use cases and for the people who wish to have more command over the model's internal functions.

Chapter 3: Building your first model

Building your most memorable AI model is a thrilling move toward the universe of computerised reasoning. To get everything rolling, I'll give you a fundamental aid on building a basic managed learning model utilising Python and the famous library sci-kit-learn. We'll make a clear model for paired grouping utilising the popular Iris dataset.

Stage 1: Introduce Required Libraries

Guarantee you have Python introduced, and use 'pip' to introduce scikit-learn, a strong library for AI in Python.

'''bash

pip install sci-kit-learn

'''

Stage 2: Import Fundamental Libraries

'''python

import numpy as np

from sklearn.datasets import load_iris

from sklearn.model_selection import train_test_split

from sklearn.preprocessing import StandardScaler

from sklearn.svm import SVC

from sklearn.metrics import accuracy_score

'''

Stage 3: load and prepare Data

In this model, we'll utilise the Iris dataset, which is incorporated into sci-kit-learn. It's a straightforward dataset with highlights like sepal length, sepal width, petal length, and petal width, used to group iris blossoms into three species. For this model, we'll improve on it in parallel order by picking two of the three classes.

'''python

Load the Iris dataset

Tensor machine learning

```
data = load_iris()
```

Select two of the three classes (Setosa and Versicolor) for binary classification

```
X = data.data[:100] # Features
```

```
y = data.target[:100] # labels
```

'''

Stage 4: Split Information into Preparing and Testing Sets

Part your dataset into two sections: a preparation set and a testing set. The preparation set is utilized to prepare the model, and the testing set is utilized to assess its exhibition.

'''python

```
X_train, X_test, y_train, y_test = train_test_split(X, y, test_size=0.2, random_state=42)
```

'''

Stage 5: Element Scaling (Optional)

Much of the time, it's essential to scale or standardise your information to guarantee that each component contributes similarly to the model's preparation. For this model, we'll utilise normalisation.

'''python

```
scaler = StandardScaler()
```

```
X_train = scaler.fit_transform(X_train)
```

```
X_test = scaler.transform(X_test)
```

'''

Stage 6: Form the Model

We'll utilise a straightforward Help Vector Machine (SVM) classifier for our paired order task. You can browse different calculations depending on your concern.

'''python

```
model = SVC(kernel='linear', C=1)
```

'''

Stage 7: Train the Model

Train your model on the preparation information.

'''python

```
model.fit(X_train, y_train)
```

'''

Stage 8: Make Prediction

Utilise the prepared model to make expectations on the testing information.

'''python

```
y_pred = model.predict(X_test)
```

'''

Stage 9: Assess the Model

Survey the model's presentation utilising assessment measurements. For parallel order, normal measurements incorporate exactness, accuracy, review, and F1-score. Here, we'll utilise precision.

'''python

```
precision = accuracy_score(y_test, y_pred)
print(f' Accuracy: {accuracy:.2f}')
```

'''

Stage 10: Make Forecasts on New Information (Optional)

When you have a prepared model, you can utilise it to make expectations on new, inconspicuous information.

In conclusion, This is a worked-on instance of building your most memorable AI model. By and by, true ventures frequently include more complicated datasets, preprocessing, hyperparameter tuning, and cross-approval. As you progress, you can investigate further developed models and procedures, however beginning with this straightforward model is an extraordinary method for getting active involvement with the universe of AI.

Linear regression with tensorflow

Straight relapse is one of the crucial calculations in AI and can be carried out utilising TensorFlow, a famous profound learning library. In this model, we'll make a straightforward direct relapse model utilising TensorFlow to foresee an objective variable because of at least one information highlight.

Stage 1: Introduce TensorFlow

Ensure you have TensorFlow introduced. You can introduce it by employing pip:

'''bash

pip introduce tensorflow

'''

Stage 2: Import Fundamental Libraries

'''python

import numpy as np

import tensorflow as tf

import matplotlib.pyplot as plt

'''

Stage 3: Create Test Data

Make some example information for preparing our straight relapse model. In this model, we'll utilise a straightforward one-layered direct relationship.

'''python

Create arbitrary information

np.random.seed(0)

X = 2 * np.random.rand(100, 1)

y = 4 + 3 * X + np.random.rand(100, 1)

'''

Stage 4: Characterise the Model

Make a straight relapse model. In TensorFlow, this is commonly done utilising the Consecutive Programming interface.

'''python

```
model = tf.keras.models.Sequential([

tf.keras.layers.Dense(1, input_shape=(1,))

])
```

'''

Stage 5: Accumulate the Model

Accumulate the model by determining the misfortune capability and advancement calculation.

'''python

```
model.compile(optimizer='sgd', loss='mean_squared_error')
```

'''

Here, we're utilising stochastic angle plunge (SGD) as the streamlining calculation and mean squared mistake as the misfortune capability.

Stage 6: Train the Model

Train the model with the example information. We'll determine the quantity of ages (emphasis on the dataset) and give the preparation information.

'''python

```
model.fit(X, y, epochs=100)
```

'''

Stage 7: Make Predictions

Utilise the prepared model to make forecasts. In this model, we'll make expectations on similar information we utilised for preparing.

'''python

```
y_pred = model.predict(X)
```

'''

Stage 8: Imagine the Results

Plot the first information and the relapse line produced by the model.

'''python

```
plt.scatter(X, y, label='Original Information')

plt.plot(X, y_pred, 'r', label='Fitted Line')

plt.xlabel('X')

plt.ylabel('y')

plt.legend()

plt.show()

'''
```

Stage 9: Utilise the Model for Predictions

You can utilise your prepared straight relapse model to make forecasts on new information by calling 'model.predict(new_data)'.

This model shows how to make a straightforward direct relapse model utilising TensorFlow. By and by, you can apply straight relapse to different issues, including foreseeing house costs, stock costs, or any circumstance where you need to display a direct connection between factors. As you advance, you can investigate more perplexing relapse models and procedures in TensorFlow.

Strategic relapse and characterization

Strategic relapse is a central factual model that is broadly utilised for grouping undertakings in AI. It is fundamental for double and multi-class grouping issues where you want to anticipate straight-out results in light of information highlights. How about we plunge into calculated relapse and grouping?

Strategic Relapse

Strategic Capability (Sigmoid)

Calculated relapse uses the strategic capability, frequently alluded to as the sigmoid capability. This capability maps any contribution to the reach somewhere in the range of 0 and 1, which is great for demonstrating probabilities:

![Sigmoid Function]

Tensor machine learning

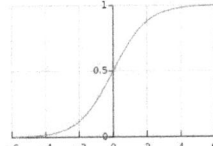
px-Calculated curve.svg.png)

The equation for the sigmoid capability is:

'''

$$\sigma(z) = 1/(1 + e^{(-z)})$$

'''

Here, 'z' is a direct blend of information highlights and their related loads.

Model Condition

The strategic relapse model takes the following structure:

'''

$$P(Y=1|X) = \sigma(\beta_0 + \beta_1 X_1 + \beta_2 X_2 + ... + \beta_\square X_\square)$$

'''

Where:

- 'P(Y=1|X)' is the likelihood of the parallel result 'Y' being 1 given input 'X'.

- 'σ' addresses the sigmoid capability.

- '$\beta_0, \beta_1, \beta_2, ...$' are the model boundaries (loads).

- '$X_0, X_1, X_2, ...$' are the information highlights.

The choice limit of the calculated relapse model is where 'P(Y=1|X)' rises to 0.5.

Twofold Order

In parallel grouping, calculated relapse is utilised to foresee one of two classes (0 or 1) in light of the info highlights. For example, it very well may be utilised for assignments like spam email recognition, illness determination, or feeling examination. The model's result is deciphered as the likelihood of the information having a place with class 1, and a limit (typically 0.5) is utilised to settle on twofold choices.

Logistic regression and classification

Calculated relapse is a key measurable model that is broadly utilised for characterization undertakings in AI. It is fundamental for parallel and multi-class characterization issues where you want to anticipate all-out results in light of information highlights. How about we plunge into strategic relapse and arrangement?

Calculated Capability (Sigmoid)

Calculated relapse uses the strategic capability, frequently alluded to as the sigmoid capability. This capability maps any contribution to the reach somewhere in the range of 0 and 1, which is great for displaying probabilities:

The recipe for the sigmoid capability is:

'''

$$\sigma(z) = 1/(1 + e^{\wedge}(- z))$$

'''

Here, 'z' is a straight mix of information highlights and their related loads.

Model Condition

The calculated relapse model takes the structure:

'''

$$P(Y=1|X) = \sigma(\beta_0 + \beta_1 X_1 + \beta_2 X_2 + ... + \beta_\Box X_\Box)$$

'''

Where:

- 'P(Y=1|X)' is the likelihood of the twofold result 'Y' being 1 given input 'X'.

- 'σ' addresses the sigmoid capability.

- 'β_0, β_1, β_2, ...' are the model boundaries (loads).

- 'X_0, X_1, X_2, ...' are the information highlights.

The choice limit of the strategic relapse model is where 'P(Y=1|X)' rises to 0.5.

Parallel Arrangement

In parallel grouping, strategic relapse is utilised to foresee one of two classes (0 or 1) because of the info highlights. For example, it tends to be utilised for assignments like spam email recognition, sickness determination, or opinion examination. The model's result is deciphered as the likelihood of the info having a place with class 1, and a limit (normally 0.5) is utilised to settle on double choices.

Multi-Class Characterization

Strategic relapse can be stretched out to deal with multi-class characterization issues, where there are multiple classes. There are two normal methodologies:

1. Softmax Relapse (Multinomial Calculated

Regression): In this strategy, you have one calculated relapse model for each class. The softmax capability is utilised to standardise the scores, giving the likelihood of dissemination over all classes. The class with the most noteworthy likelihood is the anticipated class.

2. One-versus Every one of them (One-versus Rest): This approach makes a twofold calculated relapse model for each class, where the objective class is treated as the positive class and any remaining classes as the negative class. The model that yields the most elevated likelihood decides the anticipated class.

Preparing and Advancement

The calculated relapse model is prepared involving streamlining procedures to track down the ideal qualities for the model boundaries (loads). Normal advancement calculations incorporate slope plummet and its variations. The goal is to limit a misfortune capability, frequently the cross-entropy misfortune, which estimates the disparity between the anticipated probabilities and the genuine marks.

Assessment

To assess the presentation of a calculated relapse model, a few measurements can be utilized, for example, exactness, accuracy, review, F1-score, and the region under the collector working trademark bend (AUC-ROC). These measurements give experiences into the model's capacity to accurately group occurrences and its capacity to control the compromise between accuracy and review.

In conclusion, Calculated relapse is a strong model for grouping undertakings, and it fills in as a primary idea in AI. It's fundamental for both paired and multi-class order issues, and it very well may be utilised in different true applications. Understanding calculated relapse is an essential step for anybody working in the field of AI and information science.

Neural networks with tensorflow

Brain networks are at the core of profound learning and can be carried out utilising the TensorFlow library. TensorFlow is a well-known open-source AI structure created by Google that gives an adaptable and proficient stage for building and preparing brain organisations. In this outline, I'll give an undeniable level of aid in making brain networks with TensorFlow.

Stage 1: Introduce TensorFlow

Before you start, ensure you have TensorFlow introduced. You can introduce it through pip:

'''slam

pip introduce tensorflow

'''

Stage 2: Import Vital Libraries

'''python

import tensorflow as tf

from tensorflow import keras

'''

Stage 3: Burden and Preprocess Data

Brain networks require information for preparing and testing. Load and preprocess your information utilising libraries like NumPy or TensorFlow's datasets.

Stage 4: Form the Brain Organization Model

You can make a brain network model utilising TensorFlow's significant-level Keras Programming interface. Keras is incorporated into TensorFlow and works on the method involved with building and preparing brain organisations.

Here is an essential instance of building a basic feedforward brain organisation:

'''python

model = keras.Sequential([

keras.layers.Input(shape=input_shape), # Characterise the info layer with input shape

keras.layers.Dense(64, activation='relu'), # First secret layer with 64 neurons and ReLU initiation keras.layers.Dense(32, activation='relu'), # Second secret layer with 32 neurons and ReLU actuation

keras.layers.Dense(output_units, activation='softmax') # Result layer with fitting actuation

'''

You can redo the design of your brain network by adding different sorts of layers, for example, Conv2D for convolutional layers or LSTM for repetitive layers, contingent upon your concern.

Stage 5: Gather the Model

Before preparing, you want to aggregate your model. This step includes determining the misfortune capability, analyzer, and measurements for assessing the model's presentation.

'''python

model.compile(optimizer='adam', # Pick a streamlining agent (e.g., Adam)

loss='categorical_crossentropy', # Indicate the misfortune capability (e.g., for characterization)

metrics=['accuracy']) # Characterise assessment measurements (e.g., exactness)

'''

Stage 6: Train the Model

Train the brain network model on your information utilising the 'fit' technique. Indicate the preparation information, group size, number of ages, and approval information.

'''python

history = model.fit(X_train, y_train, batch_size=32, epochs=10, validation_data=(X_val, y_val))

'''

You can screen preparing progress utilising the 'history' object, which contains misfortune and metric qualities.

Stage 7: Assess and Make Predictions

In the wake of preparing, you can assess the model's presentation on a test dataset and make forecasts.

'''python

```
test_loss, test_accuracy = model.evaluate(X_test, y_test)

expectations = model.predict(X_new_data)

'''
```

Stage 8: Calibrating and Optimization

To work on the model's presentation, you can calibrate hyperparameters, change the engineering, and apply strategies like dropout, cluster standardisation, and early halting.

Stage 9: Save and Convey the Model

You can save your prepared model utilising TensorFlow's model serialisation techniques and send it to your applications.

In conclusion, This significant level outline gives a fundamental manual for making brain networks with TensorFlow. As you progress, you can investigate more intricate designs, handle explicit errands like picture acknowledgment or regular language handling, and tweak models for further developed execution. TensorFlow's broad documentation and local area support make it an integral asset for profound learning and brain network improvement.

Chapter 4: Deep Learning

Profound learning is a subfield of AI that spotlights the utilisation of counterfeit brain organisations, especially profound brain organisations, for tackling complex issues. Profound learning has acquired monstrous prevalence and has prompted huge progressions in different areas, including PC vision, normal language handling, discourse acknowledgment, and support learning.

Here are key parts of profound learning:

1. Neural Networks: At the centre of profound learning are counterfeit brain organisations, which are enlivened by the design and capability of the human mind. These organisations comprise layers of interconnected hubs (neurons) that cycle and change information. Profound brain networks have many secret layers, permitting them to show complex connections in information.

2. Deep versus Shallow: Profound gaining separates itself from conventional AI by utilising profound brain networks with various secret layers. This profundity empowers the organisations to learn various levelled portrayals of information. Shallow models, conversely, have a set number of layers.

3. Learning Representations: One of the critical qualities of profound learning is its capacity to gain significant portrayals from crude information. In picture acknowledgment, for example, lower layers could learn essential highlights like edges, while higher layers learn complex shapes or items.

4. Unsupervised and Regulated Learning: Profound learning can be utilised for both administered and unaided learning undertakings. In managed learning, brain networks are prepared on named information to make expectations. In unaided learning, networks uncover examples and designs inside unlabeled information, frequently for errands like grouping or dimensionality decrease.

5. Big Data: Profound learning models require significant measures of information for preparation. This is because profound organisations have an enormous number of boundaries, and a huge dataset forestalls overfitting. The accessibility of enormous information plays a huge impact in the outcome of profound learning.

6. Loss Functions: The decision of a misfortune capability is critical for preparing profound learning models. Normal misfortune capabilities incorporate mean squared mistakes for relapse undertakings and cross-entropy for arrangement assignments.

7. Backpropagation: Preparing profound brain networks includes the backpropagation calculation, which changes the model's boundaries (loads and inclinations) to limit the picked misfortune capability. Inclination plummet is regularly used to streamline these boundaries.

8. Convolutional Brain Organizations (CNNs): CNNs are a kind of profound brain network intended for handling matrix-like information, like pictures. They use convolutional layers to learn picture highlights, making them profoundly compelling in PC vision assignments.

9. Recurrent Brain Organizations (RNNs): RNNs are specific for succession information, like normal language or time-series information. They have memory units that can catch conditions across time steps.

10. Transfer Learning: Move learning is a procedure where pre-prepared profound learning models are utilised as a beginning stage for new undertakings. This approach saves time and assets, also prepared models can be tweaked for explicit applications.

11. Deep Support Learning: Profound learning is likewise utilised in support realising, where specialists figure out how to pursue choices in a climate to expand a prize. Profound support learning has accomplished striking outcomes in regions like game playing and advanced mechanics.

12. Ethical Considerations: Profound learning has raised moral worries, especially in issues connected with predisposition in man-made intelligence frameworks, security, and straightforwardness. Specialists and experts are dealing with tending to these worries.

Profound learning has prompted critical forward leaps in different fields, including picture and discourse acknowledgment, language interpretation, independent vehicles, and medical services. As the field keeps on developing, it holds an extraordinary commitment to taking care of intricate and testing issues across many applications.

Convolutional neural networks (CNNs)

Convolutional Neural Networks (CNNs) are a class of profound brain networks explicitly intended for handling matrix-like information, like pictures and recordings. They have reformed the field of PC vision and are generally utilised for undertakings like picture grouping, object identification, and facial acknowledgment, and that's only the tip of the iceberg. CNNs are portrayed by their capacity to consequently gain various levelled highlights from information, making them exceptionally viable in catching examples and designs inside pictures.

Here are the critical ideas and parts of Convolutional Brain Organizations:

1. Convolutional Layers: These are the structure blocks of CNNs. Convolution tasks include applying a channel (likewise called a piece) to an info picture to remove nearby highlights. Channels slide over the information picture, and at each position, they register a weighted

amount of neighbouring pixels. This activity helps the organisation consequently distinguish edges, surfaces, and basic examples.

2. Pooling Layers: Pooling layers are many times used to diminish the spatial elements of the component maps created by convolutional layers. Max pooling and normal pooling are normal procedures, where the greatest or normal worth in a nearby locale is held, while the rest are disposed of. This decreases the computational intricacy and spotlights the most useful highlights.

3. Activation Functions: Non-direct actuation capabilities, like ReLU (Amended Straight Unit), are applied to the results of convolutional and pooling layers. These capabilities bring nonlinearity into the model and assist the organisation with learning complex connections in information.

4. Fully Associated Layers: After a few convolutional and pooling layers, completely associated layers are utilised to perform characterization. These layers level the high-layered maps into a vector and afterward, apply at least one thick layer for making expectations. This last piece of the organisation frequently incorporates a result layer with softmax initiation for multi-class arrangement undertakings.

5. Stride and Padding: Step and cushioning are hyperparameters that control the spatial elements of component maps during convolution tasks. Step decides how much the channel moves among estimations, and cushioning adds additional pixels to the contribution to guarantee the result has the ideal spatial aspects.

6. Depth and Number of Filters: CNNs comprise various convolutional layers, each with an alternate number of channels. The profundity of the organisation addresses the number of layers, and the quantity of channels in each layer decides the intricacy and limits of the organisation.

7. Transfer Learning: Move learning is a strong method where pre-prepared CNN models, such as VGG, ResNet, or Commencement, are utilised as a beginning stage for new undertakings. The lower layers of these models have learned fundamental highlights that can be significant for different PC vision errands. Calibrating these models for explicit applications can save time and assets.

8. Data Augmentation: Information expansion methods, like turn, flipping, and scaling, are frequently applied to the preparation of information to expand the size and variety of the dataset. Information expansion works on the model's speculation.

Convolutional Brain Organizations have made wonderful progress in different PC vision errands, including picture order, object recognition, picture division, and, surprisingly, more complicated undertakings like picture subtitling. They are a basic innovation in fields like independent vehicles, medical services, and reconnaissance. As the field of profound learning keeps on developing, CNNs stay at the very front of picture-related applications.

Recurrent neural networks (RNNs)

Recurrent neural networks(RNNs) are a class of counterfeit brain networks intended for dealing with grouping information. Not at all like customary feedforward brain organisations, RNNs have circles or intermittent associations, permitting them to endure data across various time steps. This ability makes RNNs especially appropriate for undertakings including successive information, for example, normal language handling, discourse acknowledgment, and time series investigation, and that's just the beginning.

Key ideas and parts of Recurrent neural networks (RNNs) include:

1. Recurrent Connections: RNNs are portrayed by intermittent associations, which empower them to keep a concealed express that catches data from past time steps. This secret state fills in as the organisation's memory, permitting it to deal with arrangements of shifting lengths.

2. Time Steps: RNNs process information successively, one step at a time. At each time step, the organisation takes information, creates a result, and updates its secret state in light of the ongoing info and the past secret state.

3. Hidden State: The secret state at each time step is a vector that encodes data from past time steps. It goes about as a type of memory that the organisation can use to comprehend and produce groupings.

4. Vanishing Inclination Problem: RNNs are defenceless to the evaporating angle issue, which impedes the preparation of profound organisations. It happens when angles become excessively little during backpropagation through time, keeping the organisation from learning long-range conditions. This issue has prompted the improvement of further developed RNN variations.

5. Long Momentary Memory (LSTM) and Gated Repetitive Unit (GRU): To address the disappearing slope issue, further developed RNN designs have been presented. LSTMs and GRUs are well-known variations that consolidate gating systems to more readily catch and oversee long-haul conditions in arrangements.

6. Applications: RNNs are utilised in a large number of uses, including:

- Normal Language Handling (NLP): RNNs are utilised for assignments like language demonstrating, machine interpretation, feeling examination, and text age.

- Discourse Recognition: RNNs can decipher communicated language into text and have applications in menial helpers, and record administrations, and that's just the beginning.

- Time Series Analysis: RNNs are utilised to anticipate and break down time series information, like stock costs, climate information, and sensor readings.

- Generative Modelling: RNNs can produce groupings, like music, text, and pictures.

- Successive Information Analysis: RNNs are applied in undertakings like video examination, penmanship acknowledgment, and DNA grouping investigation.

7. Bi-directional RNNs: notwithstanding standard RNNs that cycle information consecutively from past to future, bi-directional RNNs process information in the two headings. This helps catch relevant data from both the past and future.

8. Sequence-to-Grouping Models: RNNs are much of the time utilised in arrangement-to-succession models, where one RNN (the encoder) processes an information succession, and another RNN (the decoder) creates a result arrangement. This engineering is utilised in machine interpretation and text synopsis.

9. Attention Mechanisms: Consideration instruments have been coordinated with RNNs to permit models to zero in on unambiguous pieces of information grouping while producing a result. This has prompted upgrades in errands like machine interpretation.

While RNNs have been demonstrated to be powerful for some succession-related errands, they have their constraints, for example, trouble in catching extremely lengthy reach conditions and computational failure in parallelization. Accordingly, specialists keep on growing new designs and procedures, for example, Transformer models, which have acquired noticeable quality in the field of NLP. In any case, RNNs stay a crucial structure block for consecutive information handling and are important in different applications.

Transfer learning and pre-trained models

Move learning and pre-prepared models are strong methods in the field of AI and profound discoveries that empower you to use information obtained from one undertaking to work on the exhibition of one more related task. These techniques save time, information, and assets, making them important in different applications.

Here is an outline of move learning and pre-prepared models:

Move Learning:

Move learning is an AI method where a model created for one errand is reused as the beginning stage for a model on a subsequent undertaking. Rather than preparing a model without any preparation, you start with a pre-prepared model and tweak it for your particular issue.

The vital stages in move learning are as per the following:

1. Select a Pre-prepared Model: Pick a pre-prepared model that has been prepared on an enormous and significant dataset. Normal pre-prepared models incorporate VGG, ResNet, Beginning, and BERT for different assignments.

2. Remove the Top Layers: Normally, you eliminate the top layers (yield layers) of the pre-prepared model, which are well-defined for the first assignment, and hold the lower layers that have learned helpful highlights.

3. Add New Layers: Add new layers, frequently tweaked for your particular errand, on top of the lower layers. These new layers might incorporate result layers that match the number of classes in your concern.

4. Fine-tune the Model: Train the model utilising your information, beginning with the loads gained from the pre-prepared model. This step is many times more effective and quicker than preparing without any preparation.

Advantages of Move Learning:

1. Improved Performance: Move to gain permits you to use information gained from a huge dataset, which can essentially support the presentation of your model, particularly when you have restricted information.

2. Reduced Preparing Time: Preparing just the top layers of a model is commonly quicker than preparing a profound brain network without any preparation.

3. Less Information Requirement: Move learning can function admirably with more modest datasets, making it relevant in situations where it is trying to gather a lot of information.

4. Generalisation: Pre-prepared models have proactively learned helpful highlights, elevating better speculation to new information.

Pre-prepared Models:

Pre-prepared models are brain network models that have been prepared on huge datasets and have accomplished cutting-edge execution in different assignments. These models act as a beginning stage for move learning and are accessible in famous profound learning libraries like TensorFlow and PyTorch.

A few broadly utilised pre-prepared models include:

1. ImageNet Pre-prepared Models: These models are prepared on the ImageNet dataset, an enormous assortment of marked pictures. They incorporate structures like VGG, ResNet, Commencement, and MobileNet.

2. BERT (Bidirectional Encoder Portrayals from Transformers): BERT is a pre-prepared model for regular language handling undertakings. It altogether affects undertakings like message grouping, opinion examination, and question-responding.

3. GPT (Generative Pre-prepared Transformer): GPT models are intended for undertakings connected with text age and understanding. They are famous for text age, language display, and interpretation undertakings.

4. YOLO (You Just Look Once): Consequences be damned is a pre-prepared model for ongoing item discovery in pictures and recordings.

5. OpenAI's GPT-3: GPT-3 is a profoundly progressed language model that can play out an extensive variety of language-related errands.

Utilising pre-prepared models, you can save time and assets by tweaking these models for your particular assignment. Move learning with pre-prepared models has turned into a standard practice in AI and profound learning and is material to a wide cluster of issues in PC vision, normal language handling, discourse acknowledgment, and then some.

Chapter 5: Advanced topics

here are a few high-level points in the field of AI and profound discovering that have acquired unmistakable quality as of late and keep on driving development and examination:

1. Generative Ill-disposed Organisations (GANs): GANs are a class of profound learning models that comprise a generator and a discriminator, prepared together extremely. GANs are utilised for picture age, style movement, picture picture-to-picture interpretation, and that's just the beginning.

2. Reinforcement Learning: Support learning includes preparing specialists to settle on a succession of choices to expand a combined prize. This field has seen huge progressions, with applications in advanced mechanics, game playing, and independent frameworks.

3. Self-Managed Learning: Self-directed gaining is a preparation worldview where models gain from information without unequivocal names. It has been utilized for assignments like portrayal learning and language demonstration.

4. Transformers: Transformers are a kind of profound brain network engineering that has changed normal language handling. Models like BERT and GPT-3 depend on Transformer engineering and have set new benchmarks in NLP.

5. Explainable artificial intelligence (XAI): Getting it and making sense of the choices made by AI models is turning out to be progressively significant. XAI research intends to make artificial intelligence models more straightforward and interpretable.

6. Federated Learning: Combined learning is a protection safeguarding strategy that permits model preparation across various decentralised gadgets or servers without trading crude information. It's important in medical care and other delicate spaces.

7. AI Morals and Fairness: The moral utilisation of computer-based intelligence and guaranteeing decency in artificial intelligence frameworks are basic subjects. Analysts and associations are effectively resolving issues connected with predisposition, decency, straightforwardness, and responsibility in man-made intelligence.

8. Meta-Learning: Meta-learning centres around preparing models to figure out how to learn. These models can adjust to new errands with not many models, making them profoundly adaptable.

9. Graph Brain Networks: GNNs are intended to work with diagram-organised information, making them helpful for interpersonal organisation examination, suggestion frameworks, and science-related assignments.

10. Neuromorphic Computing: Neuromorphic equipment and programming intend to copy the design and capability of the human mind. This has applications in tangible handling, advanced mechanics, and mental figuring.

11. Quantum Machine Learning: Quantum figuring holds a guarantee for tackling complex issues quicker, and quantum AI investigates the joining of quantum registering with AI calculations.

12. Edge AI: Running AI models anxious gadgets, like IoT gadgets or cell phones, are building up forward movement. It empowers constant handling and decision-production at the wellspring of information.

13. AI in Healthcare: artificial intelligence is making huge commitments to medical care, including finding, drug revelation, patient observation, and customised medication.

14. AI in Finance: The monetary business is taking on simulated intelligence for extortion recognition, risk appraisal, algorithmic exchanging, and client assistance.

15. AI in Independent Vehicles: Self-driving vehicles and robots depend on simulated intelligence for discernment, navigation, and control frameworks.

16. AI in Creativity: simulated intelligence is utilised in craftsmanship, music, and content age, including artificial intelligence-produced workmanship, music pieces, and composing.

These high-level points address areas of dynamic innovative work, where state-of-the-art advancements are pushing the limits of what is conceivable in AI and computerised reasoning. Remaining informed about these subjects and their potential applications is fundamental for those functioning in the field and for understanding how man-made intelligence is moulding different enterprises and spaces.

Autoencoders and generative adversarial networks (GANs):

Autoencoders and Generative Ill-disposed Organisations (GANs) are two strong procedures in the profound discovery that are frequently utilised for various purposes, however, both are connected with generative displaying.

Autoencoders:

Autoencoders are a kind of brain network engineering utilised for solo learning, information pressure, highlight learning, and denoising. They comprise two principal parts: an encoder and a decoder. The objective of an autoencoder is to become familiar with a minimal portrayal of info information by encoding it into a lower-layered inactive space and afterward translating it back to the first information. Autoencoders can be classified into a few kinds, including:

1. Vanilla Autoencoders: These have a solitary bottleneck layer in the centre that addresses the packed portrayal of the info information. They are utilised for errands like dimensionality decrease and sound decrease.

2. Variational Autoencoders (VAEs): VAEs are a probabilistic variation of autoencoders. They become familiar with a compacted portrayal as well as produce a likelihood dispersion over potential portrayals, considering a more adaptable age of information. VAEs are frequently utilised for generative undertakings.

3. Denoising Autoencoders: These are prepared to eliminate commotion or defilement from input information, making them valuable for information denoising and information attribution.

Generative Ill-disposed Organisations (GANs):

GANs are a kind of generative model that comprises two brain organisations: a generator and a discriminator. They are prepared thoughtfully. The generator endeavours to make information tests that are vague from genuine information, while the discriminator expects to differentiate between genuine and created information. GANs are utilised for creating new, sensible information tests and have been applied to different spaces, including:

1. Image Generation: GANs have been utilised to produce photorealistic pictures, workmanship, and even deep fake pictures and recordings.

2. Style Transfer: GANs can be utilised to move the style of one picture to another, like changing the imaginative style of a composition or applying the presence of one photo to another.

3. Super-Resolution: GANs can improve the goal and detail of pictures, which is significant in assignments like upscaling low-goal photographs.

4. Image-to-Picture Translation: GANs are utilised for errands like switching high-contrast pictures over completely to variety, transforming draws into reasonable pictures, or changing day scenes to night scenes.

5. Text-to-Picture Synthesis: GANs can produce pictures from text portrayals, empowering text-based picture amalgamation.

GANs have additionally led to different models and augmentations, like Profound Convolutional GANs (DCGANs), Contingent GANs (cGANs), and Moderate GANs.

Key Differences:

- Autoencoders are principally utilised for information pressure, including learning, and information reproduction, while GANs are intended for the information age.

- Autoencoders gain planning from input information to a lower-layered portrayal and back, expecting to limit reproduction misfortune. GANs centre around antagonistic preparation to produce information tests that are unclear from genuine information.

- Autoencoders can be utilised for undertakings like denoising, dimensionality decrease, and information ascription. GANs succeed in picture age, style move, and super-goal.

- Autoencoders have a deterministic encoder and decoder, while GANs have a generator and discriminator prepared in a game-like setting.

Both autoencoders and GANs assume significant parts in the field of profound learning and have assorted applications in different areas. The decision between them relies upon the particular undertaking and objectives of the model.

Reinforcement learning with tensorflow

Support learning with TensorFlow is a famous methodology for creating and preparing support learning specialists. TensorFlow is a flexible profound learning system that can be utilised for different AI undertakings, including support learning. Here are the fundamental stages to get everything rolling:

1. Installation: First, guarantee you have TensorFlow introduced. You can utilise 'pip' to introduce it:

'''

pip install tensorflow

'''

2. Environment Setup: Establish the climate or recreation for your RL issue. You can involve libraries like OpenAI Exercise Center to set up conditions for testing and preparing RL specialists.

3. Define Your Model: Construct a brain network model utilising TensorFlow to address your RL specialist. This model will take perceptions from the climate and result activities.

4. Choose an RL Algorithm: There are different RL calculations like Q-Learning, Profound Q-Organizations (DQN), Proximal Approach Improvement (PPO), and that's just the beginning. Pick the one that suits your concern.

5. Training Loop: Execute the preparation circle, where the specialist associates with the climate, gathers information (perceptions, activities, rewards), and updates its arrangement in light of the picked RL calculation.

6. Loss Capability and Optimization: Characterise a misfortune capability that evaluates how well the specialist is performing. Utilise TensorFlow's analyzers to limit this misfortune and work on the specialist's strategy.

7. Exploration versus Exploitation: Carry out a procedure for the specialist to investigate the climate and learn ideal strategies while taking advantage of its ongoing information.

8. Evaluation: Occasionally assess the specialist's exhibition in the climate to keep tabs on its development.

9. Hyperparameter Tuning: Tweak hyperparameters like learning rate, markdown component, and organisation design to enhance preparation.

10. Save and Deploy: When the specialist is prepared, save the model boundaries and send it for certifiable applications.

Here is a straightforward illustration of how to make a DQN specialist utilising TensorFlow:

```python
import tensorflow as tf

from tensorflow import keras

import gym

Make a DQN model

model = keras.Sequential([

keras. layers.Dense(24, input_shape=(state_size,), activation='relu'),

Keras. layers.Dense(24, activation='relu'),

keras. layers.Dense(action_size, activation='linear')


Characterise the enhancer and misfortune capability

streamlining agent = tf.keras.optimizers.Adam(learning_rate=0.001)

model.compile(loss='mse', optimizer=optimizer)

Preparing circle and specialist climate connection

for episode in range(num_episodes):

state = env.reset()
```

```
done = False

while not done:

# Specialist chooses an activity

action = model.predict(state)

# Execute the action in the environment

next_state, reward, done, _ = env.step(action)

# Update the model because of the experience

# ...

Save the prepared model for some time in the future

model. Save ('dqn_model.h5')

'''
```

This is a worked-on model, and RL can be very complicated. You would have to adjust it to your particular issue and RL calculation. Also, consider utilising libraries like TensorFlow Specialists (tf-specialists) to smooth out RL improvement with TensorFlow.

Natural language processing with Tensorflow

Normal Language Handling (NLP) with TensorFlow is a strong methodology for creating applications that comprehend, decipher, and produce human language. TensorFlow offers different instruments and assets to chip away at NLP errands. Here is an essential diagram of how to get everything rolling with NLP in TensorFlow:

1. Installation: Guarantee you have TensorFlow introduced:

```
'''

pip install tensorflow

''›
```

2. Text Preprocessing: Set up your text information by tokenizing, cleaning, and vectorizing it. TensorFlow gives devices to these undertakings, for example the 'Tokenizer' and 'TextVectorization' layers.

3. Choose NLP Model: Select the NLP model design because of your errand. Normal decisions incorporate Repetitive Brain Organizations (RNNs), Long Momentary Memory (LSTM) organisations, Transformer models (like BERT or GPT), and then some.

4. Embeddings: Utilise pre-prepared word embeddings like Word2Vec, GloVe, or TensorFlow Center's embeddings, or train custom embeddings for your particular undertaking.

5. Model Building: Make an NLP model utilising TensorFlow's Keras Programming interface. Characterise the model engineering, including the installing layer, repetitive layers, consideration instruments, and result layers because of your NLP issue.

6. Training: Set up your named dataset and use it to prepare your NLP model. Characterise proper misfortune capabilities (e.g., downright cross-entropy for characterization assignments) and analyzers.

7. Fine-Tuning: For huge-scope language models like BERT or GPT, calibrating your particular assignment is often vital. TensorFlow's Embracing Face Transformers library can be useful for this reason.

8. Evaluation: Assess the model's exhibition on approval or test information utilising important measurements, for example, precision, F1-score, or perplexity, contingent upon your assignment.

9. Inference: Utilise the prepared NLP model to make expectations or produce text in light of new info information.

10. Save and Deploy: Save the prepared model and convey it in your application or administration.

Here is an improved instance of preparing a text grouping model with TensorFlow:

'''python

import tensorflow as tf

from tensorflow import keras

Define and assemble the NLP model

model = keras.Sequential([

keras. layers.Embedding(input_dim=vocab_size, output_dim=embed_dim, input_length=max_seq_length),

keras. layers.LSTM(64),

keras. layers.Dense(1, activation='sigmoid')

])

model.compile(loss='binary_crossentropy', optimizer='adam', metrics=['accuracy'])

Tensor machine learning

Train the model

model.fit(X_train, y_train, epochs=5, batch_size=32, validation_data=(X_val, y_val))

Assess the model

Loss, precision = model.evaluate(X_test, y_test)

print(f"Test precision: {accuracy}")

'''

This model exhibits message grouping utilising an LSTM-based model, yet similar standards apply to other NLP undertakings like opinion investigation, named element acknowledgment, and machine interpretation, and that's only the tip of the iceberg. Contingent upon your particular issue, you might require further developed models and methods. TensorFlow additionally gives pre-prepared models and libraries that can fundamentally improve on NLP errands, like TensorFlow Center point, TensorFlow Text, and TensorFlow's true models for different NLP benchmarks.

Chapter 6: Training and Optimization

Preparing and improving are basic parts of AI and profound learning. The objective is to help a model to perform well on a given errand. Here is a general framework of the preparation and streamlining process:

1. Data Preparation:

- Accumulate and preprocess your information, guaranteeing it's in a reasonable configuration.

- Divide the information into preparing, approval, and test sets.

2. Select a Model:

- Pick a fitting AI or profound learning model because of the issue you're attempting to settle.

3. Loss Function:

- Characterise a misfortune capability (otherwise called an expense or goal capability) that evaluates how well the model is performing.

4. Optimization Algorithm:

- Select an improvement calculation (e.g., Stochastic Inclination Drop, Adam, RMSprop) to refresh the model's boundaries during preparation.

5. Hyperparameter Tuning:

- Tweak hyperparameters, for example, learning rate, bunch size, and regularisation solidarity to enhance preparation.

6. Training Loop:

- Emphasise the preparation information in little bunches.

- Forward pass: Register expectations utilising the ongoing model.

- Figure the misfortune utilising the picked misfortune capability.

- Backpropagation: Work out angles of the misfortune regarding model boundaries.

- Update model boundaries utilising the picked enhancer.

7. Early Stopping:

- Screen the model's presentation on the approval set.

- Carry out early halting-to-end preparation when the model's exhibition begins to corrupt.

8. Regularisation:

- Execute regularisation strategies like L1 or L2 regularisation to forestall overfitting.

9. Batch Normalisation:

- Apply group standardisation to balance out preparing and possibly accelerate intermingling.

10. Initialization:

- Utilise legitimate weight introduction methods like Xavier (Glorot) or He statement.

11. Learning Rate Scheduling:

- Execute learning rate plans (e.g., step rot, learning rate tempering) to adjust the learning rate during preparation.

12. Data Augmentation:

- If pertinent, use information expansion methods to expand the variety of preparing information and further develop speculation.

13. Monitoring:

- Log and screen different preparation measurements, including preparing misfortune, approval misfortune, and execution measurements well defined for your assignment.

14. Evaluation:

- Assess the last model on a different test dataset to evaluate its speculation execution.

15. Regular Maintenance:

- Keep up with the model by retraining it with new information intermittently.

16. Deployment:

- Send the prepared model for use in genuine applications.

The particular execution subtleties and instruments you use will rely upon the structure you're working with. TensorFlow, PyTorch, and sci-kit-learn are famous solutions for preparing and improving. Robotized hyperparameter improvement instruments like Matrix Search and Arbitrary Hunt can be useful for tuning hyperparameters. Furthermore, high-level methods like exchange learning, model refining, and combined learning might be material relying upon the issue and the size of your information.

Loss functions and Optimization

Misfortune capabilities and streamlining calculations are two central parts of the preparation cycle in AI and profound learning. We should dig further into each:

Misfortune Function:

A misfortune capability (otherwise called an expense or goal capability) gauges the contrast between the anticipated upsides of your model and the genuine objective qualities in your dataset. It measures how well the model is performing for a given arrangement of boundaries. The objective during preparation is to limit this misfortune capability.

Normal misfortune capabilities for different sorts of AI assignments include:

1. Mean Squared Blunder (MSE): Utilised for relapse issues.

2. Binary Cross-Entropy: Material for twofold characterization assignments.

3. Categorical Cross-Entropy: Utilised for multiclass characterization issues.

4. Hinge Loss: Ordinarily utilised for help vector machines and direct classifiers.

5. Log Misfortune (Strategic Loss): Appropriate for calculated relapse and probabilistic characterization errands.

6. Custom Misfortune Functions: You can plan custom misfortune capabilities custom-fitted to your particular issue.

The decision of the misfortune capability relies upon the idea of the issue you're attempting to address. Vital to select a misfortune capability that lines up with your concern's goals and the result of your model.

Enhancement Algorithm:

Enhancement calculations are liable for refreshing the model's boundaries to limit the misfortune capability. They iteratively change the model's loads and inclinations because of the slopes of the misfortune for those boundaries. Some generally utilised improvement calculations include:

1. Stochastic Inclination Drop (SGD): The exemplary enhancement calculation. It refreshes model boundaries utilising little irregular clumps of information.

2. Adam (Versatile Second Estimation): A well-known improvement calculation that joins the benefits of RMSprop and force.

3. RMSprop (Root Mean Square Propagation): Versatile learning rate technique that changes the learning rates for every boundary separately.

4. Adagrad (Versatile Inclination Algorithm): A versatile learning rate enhancement calculation.

5. LBFGS (Restricted memory Broyden-Fletcher-Goldfarb-Shanno): A semi Newton technique for enhancement.

6. Nadam (Nesterov-sped up Versatile Second Estimation): A variation of Adam with Nesterov energy.

7. Custom Optimizers: You can make custom streamlining calculations by changing inclination drop strategies.

The decision of the advancement calculation can fundamentally influence the preparation speed and the union of the model. The learning rate and other hyperparameters of the enhancer ought to be painstakingly tuned in light of your particular issue.

Practically speaking, the blend of misfortune capability and advancement calculation is critical for accomplishing great model execution. Trial and error with various mixes, and hyperparameters, and observing the preparation interaction (e.g., through learning rate plans or early halting) can prompt improved results. Famous AI libraries like TensorFlow and PyTorch give a scope of inherent misfortune capabilities and streamlining calculations, making it more straightforward to examine and track down the right arrangement for your concern.

Hyperparameter Tuning

Hyperparameter tuning, otherwise called hyperparameter streamlining, is a basic move toward AI and profound figuring out how to track down the best mix of hyperparameters for your model. Hyperparameters are settings that are not gained from the information but rather set before preparing. They incorporate learning rates, clump estimates, the number of layers, the number of neurons in each layer, and regularisation strength, and that's just the beginning. This is the way you can perform hyperparameter tuning actually:

1. Define a Hunt Space:

- Distinguish the hyperparameters you need to tune and characterise their hunt space, including the reach or values they can take. For instance, you might determine learning rates somewhere in the range of 0.001 and 0.1.

2. Choose a Pursuit Strategy:

- There are a few strategies to look at the hyperparameter space, including:

- Lattice Search: Thoroughly search all potential blends inside the characterised range.

- Arbitrary Pursuit: Haphazardly test mixes from the inquiry space.

- Bayesian Improvement: A more modern methodology that models the misfortune capability and chooses the following hyperparameters to attempt in light of the model's expectations.

3. Cross-Validation:

- Utilise cross-approval to assess the model's exhibition for each arrangement of hyperparameters. Cross-approval guarantees that the model's presentation isn't overfitted to a particular dataset split.

4. Objective Function:

- Characterise a goal capability that evaluates the model's presentation given the cross-approval results. This could be the normal approval exactness, F1 score, or some other important measurement for your errand.

5. Search and Evaluate:

- Play out the hyperparameter search in light of your picked technique, assessing the goal capability for each arrangement of hyperparameters.

6. Track Results:

- Track the outcomes for each arrangement of hyperparameters. This permits you to look at and break down the exhibition of various arrangements.

7. Iterate and Refine:

- Utilise the outcomes to settle on informed conclusions about which hyperparameters appear to appropriately work best and update your inquiry system.

8. Early Stopping:

- Execute early halting to end preparing for mixes that show little commitment during the inquiry.

9. Final Evaluation:

- In the wake of tracking down the best hyperparameters, assess the model on a different test dataset to guarantee that the hyperparameter tuning process didn't prompt overfitting on the approval information.

10. Automation:

- Consider utilising robotized hyperparameter tuning libraries like Optuna, Hyperopt, or scikit-learn's GridSearchCV and RandomizedSearchCV to smooth out the interaction.

11. Parallelize:

- On the off chance that you approach different registering assets, you can parallelize the hyperparameter search to accelerate the interaction.

12. Regularization and Component Engineering:

- Close by hyperparameter tuning, consider consolidating regularisation methods and element designing to additionally work on model execution.

Hyperparameter tuning is in many cases an iterative cycle, and there is no one size-fits-all methodology. It requires persistence and trial and error to find the best arrangement of hyperparameters for your particular AI task.

Regularisation and Dropout

Regularisation strategies, including dropout, are fundamental techniques to forestall overfitting and work on the speculation of AI and profound learning models. Here is a clarification of regularisation and how dropout functions:

Regularisation:

Regularisation is a bunch of procedures used to forestall an AI model from fitting the preparation information too intently, which can prompt overfitting. Overfitting happens when a model performs well on the preparation information yet inadequately on inconspicuous information. Two normal regularisation procedures are L1 (Rope) and L2 (Edge) regularisation:

1. L1 Regularization (Lasso):

- L1 regularisation adds punishment to the model's misfortune capability for the outright upsides of the model's loads.

- It empowers a portion of the model's loads to turn out to be precisely zero, really performing highlight determination.

- L1 regularisation is especially valuable when you suspect that a subset of highlights is fundamental.

2. L2 Regularization (Ridge):

- L2 regularisation adds a punishment to the misfortune capability for the amount of squares of the model's loads.

- It keeps the model from having extremely enormous weight values.

- L2 regularisation helps in controlling the intricacy of the model and by and large guides in forestalling overfitting.

Dropout:

Dropout is a regularisation method explicitly intended for brain organisations, including profound learning models. It was acquainted with relieving overfitting by haphazardly "exiting" (setting to nothing) an extent of neurons during each preparing emphasis. The central issues about dropout are:

1. During Training:

- During each forward and reverse pass in preparation, an irregular subset of neurons is set to zero with a predefined dropout rate (e.g., 0.5).

- This recreates preparing different "diminished" networks all the while, as every dropout activity eliminates a few neurons from the organisation.

2. During Inference:

- During deduction (while making expectations), dropout is normally switched off, and all neurons are utilised.

3. Benefits:

- Dropout assists the model with turning out to be more vigorous and keeps it from depending too intensely on any one neuron.

- It urges neurons to freely learn more helpful elements.

4. Dropout Rate:

- The dropout rate is a hyperparameter that decides the likelihood of exiting every neuron during preparation. A regular worth is 0.5, however, this can be tuned.

This is the way you can execute dropout in a profound learning model utilising TensorFlow:

```python
import tensorflow as tf

model = tf.keras.Sequential([

tf.keras.layers.Dense(128, activation='relu', input_shape=(input_dim,)),

tf.keras.layers.Dropout(0.5), # Dropout layer with a dropout pace of 0.5
```

```
tf.keras.layers.Dense(64, activation='relu'),

tf.keras.layers.Dense(output_dim, activation='softmax')

])

# Aggregate and train the model to the surprise of no one

'''
```

By consolidating dropout, you can work on the speculation of your brain organisation and make it more impervious to overfitting. The dropout rate is a hyperparameter you can change during model tuning to track down the right harmony among regularisation and model execution.

Chapter 7: Deploying models

Conveying an AI or profound learning model is the most common way of making your prepared model accessible for use in true applications. The organisation cycle can differ contingent upon your particular use case and foundation, however here are the general advances engaged with conveying a model:

1. Model Export:

- Save or commodity your prepared model to a record design that can be handily stacked and utilised in the sending climate. Normal configurations incorporate TensorFlow's SavedModel design, ONNX, or custom serialisation designs.

2. Scalability and Infrastructure:

- Figure out where you will send the model. Choices incorporate cloud administrations (e.g., AWS, Purplish Blue, Google Cloud), on-premises servers, edge gadgets, or portable applications. Guarantee that your picked foundation can deal with the model's computational prerequisites.

3. Model Serving:

- Pick a model serving arrangement or system reasonable for your sending climate. Well-known choices incorporate TensorFlow Serving, FastAPI, and Jar, and the sky is the limit from there. These structures give HTTP endpoints to making forecasts with your model.

4. API Design:

- Characterise a Programming interface that uncovered your model's usefulness. This Programming interface ought to determine input information design, reaction design, and any extra data expected for making expectations.

5. Data Preprocessing:

- Execute information preprocessing steps in your arrangement code to guarantee that input information is appropriately changed and ready for making expectations. This could incorporate standardisation, tokenization, or some other important information changes.

6. Security and Authentication:

- Carry out safety efforts to safeguard your model's Programming interface. This might include confirmation, approval, and encryption relying upon the responsiveness of your information and model.

7. Monitoring and Logging:

- Set up observing and logging to follow model execution and use progressively. This can assist you with recognizing issues and advancing your model over the long run.

8. Deployment Automation:

- Mechanize the arrangement interaction, including scaling, refreshing, and dealing with different examples of your model. Apparatuses like Docker and Kubernetes can assist with containerization and coordination.

9. Testing and Quality Assurance:

- Completely test your conveyed model to guarantee it functions true to form and handles different info situations effortlessly. Incorporate unit tests, reconciliation tests, and burden tests.

10. Documentation:

- Make clear and complete documentation for your Programming interface, including how to make demands, the normal reactions, and model use cases.

11. Versioning:

- Execute forming for your model and Programming interface to take into consideration refreshes and reverse similarity. This is significant assuming that you intend to improve or refine your model over the long haul.

12. Deployment Stage and Framework Configuration:

- Guarantee that the sending stage and foundation are designed accurately to help your model, including equipment speed increase (e.g., GPUs) and vital libraries.

13. Continuous Reconciliation/Consistent Organization (CI/CD):

- If conceivable, set up a CI/Disc pipeline to robotize testing and organisation. This can assist with smoothing out the most common way of refreshing and redeploying your model.

14. Load Adjusting and Redundancy:

- Execute load adjusting and overt repetitiveness to guarantee high accessibility and adaptation to non-critical failure, particularly for models with high utilisation or strategic applications.

15. User Criticism and Maintenance:

- Gather client criticism and screen the conveyed model's exhibition underway. Utilise this data to refine and keep up with the model after some time.

16. Compliance and Governance:

- Guarantee that your sending follows lawful and administrative prerequisites, particularly for delicate information.

Recollect that the arrangement interaction can be complicated, and the particular advances might fluctuate given your utilisation case and climate. It's fundamental to completely test and approve your conveyed model to guarantee it meets your presentation and unwavering quality prerequisites.

Exporting and serving tensorflow models

Sending out and serving TensorFlow models includes the most common way of saving your prepared TensorFlow model and making it accessible for ongoing derivation or expectations. TensorFlow gives devices and libraries to work with this. Here are the moves toward product and serve a TensorFlow model:

1. Save Your Prepared Model:

- After preparing your TensorFlow model, save it to an organisation that can be effortlessly stacked for serving. One normal configuration is the SavedModel design, which is a language-freethinker design for determining AI models.

'''python

model.save('path_to_saved_model')

'''

2. Model Commodity and Mark Definition:

- While saving the model as a SavedModel, TensorFlow naturally incorporates the vital data for signature definition. In any case, assuming that you want to alter the information and result tensors for your serving needs, you can characterise the marks unequivocally.

'''python

@tf.function(input_signature=[tf.TensorSpec(shape=[None, input_dim], dtype=tf.float32)])

def serve_model(inputs):

expectations = model(inputs)

return {'predictions': predictions}

'''

3. TensorFlow Serving:

- TensorFlow Serving is a committed model serving framework intended for serving TensorFlow models in a creation climate. You can send your SavedModel utilizing TensorFlow Serving.

'''bash

```
docker run - p 8501:8501 - - name=tf_model_serving - - mount
type=bind,source=/way/to/saved_model_directory,target=/models/model_name - e
MODEL_NAME=model_name - t tensorflow/serving
```

'''

The model will be available through HTTP endpoints.

4. TensorFlow Serving Client:

- To make forecasts or derivations, you can utilise the TensorFlow Serving client libraries or send HTTP POST demands with input information to the TensorFlow Serving REST Programming interface.

5. Other Structures and Tools:

- You can send out TensorFlow models to ONNX design for interoperability with other profound learning structures and devices. ONNX Runtime, for instance, can serve ONNX models proficiently.

6. TensorFlow Light (for Portable and Edge Devices):

- If you want to serve models on versatile or edge gadgets, you can change your TensorFlow model completely to the TensorFlow Light arrangement. TensorFlow Light is upgraded for portable and asset-obliged conditions.

7. Custom Deployment:

- If you favour custom arrangements, you can execute your model-serving framework utilising systems like Cup or FastAPI. Load the SavedModel and serve it through your Programming interface endpoints.

8. Cloud Services:

- Many cloud suppliers offer model organisation and serving administrations. For instance, Google Cloud artificial intelligence Stage, AWS SageMaker, and Purplish Blue ML can help you send and deal with your TensorFlow models at scale.

9. Model Forming and Management:

- Consider carrying out forming for your models to work with updates and upkeep. Apparatuses like TensorFlow Serving support model forming.

10. Security and Authentication:

- Execute safety efforts, like validation and approval, to safeguard your model endpoints from unapproved access.

Make sure to consider factors like execution, versatility, and asset usage while picking a sending technique. The particular methodology you take will rely upon your task's necessities and framework.

Tensorflow serving and tensorflow lite

TensorFlow Serving and TensorFlow Light are two unmistakable parts of the TensorFlow biological system, each intended for explicit organisation situations:

TensorFlow Serving:

TensorFlow Serving is a devoted model-serving framework made by TensorFlow for serving AI models in a creation climate. It is especially appropriate for serving TensorFlow models over an organisation. Here are a few vital elements and use cases for TensorFlow Serving:

1. High-Execution Model Serving: TensorFlow Serving is upgraded for serving TensorFlow models with low dormancy and high throughput.

2. Serving Any TensorFlow Model: It can serve models in the SavedModel design, which is the standard arrangement for trading prepared TensorFlow models. TensorFlow Serving is a language-freethinker, so it tends to be utilised with models worked in TensorFlow in any supported language (Python, C++, and so on.).

3. Easy Deployment: You can send TensorFlow Filling in as a Docker holder, and it gives HTTP endpoints to show deduction. This makes it simple to coordinate with different applications.

4. Model Versioning: TensorFlow Serving upholds model forming, permitting you to deal with various variants of your models and effectively switch between them.

5. Scalability: It upholds load adjusting and can be utilized in a disseminated arrangement to serve models at scale.

6. Dynamic Batching: TensorFlow Serving can deal with dynamic clustering, permitting it to improve model deduction given differing responsibilities.

TensorFlow Lite:

TensorFlow Light is a system created by TensorFlow explicitly for running AI models on asset-compelled gadgets, like cell phones and edge gadgets (IoT). Key elements and use cases for TensorFlow Light include:

1. Mobile and Edge Deployment: TensorFlow Light is intended for portable and edge gadgets where computational assets (central processor, GPU, memory) are restricted.

2. Model Optimization: It incorporates instruments for quantization and improvement of TensorFlow models, decreasing their size and further developing induction speed on cell phones.

3. Interoperability: TensorFlow Light backs different stages, including Android, iOS, and inserted frameworks. It tends to be utilized in versatile application improvement and implanted frameworks.

4. On-Gadget Inference: TensorFlow Light permits you to run AI models straightforwardly on the gadget without requiring a consistent network to a server.

5. TensorFlow Light for Microcontrollers: For incredibly asset-obsessed gadgets, TensorFlow Light for Microcontrollers is accessible, offering support for edge gadgets with negligible computational abilities.

In outline, TensorFlow Serving is principally centred around serving TensorFlow models in a creation climate where low idleness and high throughput are basic. Then again, TensorFlow Light is outfitted towards running models on versatile and edge gadgets with asset imperatives, enhancing them for on-gadget induction. The decision between them relies upon your arrangement prerequisites and target stages.

Chapter 8: Practical Applications

Both TensorFlow Serving and TensorFlow Light have reasonable applications in different spaces. Here are some certifiable use cases for each:

TensorFlow Serving:

1. E-trade Suggestion Engines: Severe profound learning proposal models to give customised item proposals to clients continuously.

2. Natural Language Handling (NLP) Services: Convey language models for chatbots and opinion examination to give intelligent and mindful reactions.

3. Computer Vision: Serve picture acknowledgment models for applications like substance balance, object discovery, and facial acknowledgment in reconnaissance frameworks.

4. Healthcare: Convey clinical picture examination models for diagnosing illnesses from clinical pictures like X-beams, X-rays, or CT filters.

5. Ad Snap Prediction: Serve models for anticipating promotion navigate rates, permitting web-based publicising stages to improve promotion focusing on.

6. Fraud Detection: Convey models for continuous misrepresentation location in monetary exchanges, assisting with forestalling false exercises.

7. Smart Assistants: Power voice-controlled shrewd colleagues with discourse acknowledgment models for understanding and answering client orders.

8. Time Series Forecasting:Serve models for anticipating monetary market patterns, weather conditions, or request gauging in the production network of the board.

TensorFlow Lite:

1. Mobile Apps: Incorporate lightweight AI models into portable applications for on-gadget picture and discourse acknowledgment, and interpretation, from there, the sky's the limit.

2. Edge Gadgets and IoT: Send model tense gadgets like sensors, cameras, and IoT gadgets for neighbourhood handling and independent direction.

3. Autonomous Vehicles: Run models for object discovery, path following, and crash evasion on independent vehicles with restricted computational assets.

4. Health Monitoring: Foster portable applications for checking well-being information, for example, pulse, ECG investigation, and fall location utilising on-gadget models.

5. Language Translation: Carry out on-gadget language interpretation for portable applications, empowering disconnected interpretation abilities.

6. Agriculture: Utilise TensorFlow Light on rambles or implanted gadgets to break down crop wellbeing, distinguish bothers, and streamline the water system.

7. Gesture Recognition: Coordinate models into wearables and gadgets to perceive signals for client connection.

8. Retail Stock Management: Send models on standardised tag scanners and rack cameras for continuous stock following and stock administration.

These are only a couple of instances of the reasonable utilizations of TensorFlow Serving and TensorFlow Light. As a general rule, TensorFlow Serving is reasonable for situations where models should be served over an organisation with low inertness and high throughput, while TensorFlow Light is great for running models on asset-compelled versatile and edge gadgets, giving on-gadget derivation capacities to many applications.

Image classification and object detection

Picture grouping and article discovery are two PC vision errands, and they have unmistakable purposes and approaches:

Picture Classification:

1. Purpose:

- Picture characterization is the errand of doling out a predefined mark or classification to a whole picture. It addresses the inquiry, "What is in this image?" by recognizing the essential article or scene class.

2. Approach:

- Picture characterization commonly utilises convolutional brain organisations (CNNs) to extricate highlights from the picture and anticipate the most probable class name in light of these elements.

- The result is a solitary class name, and the model expects to figure out which class addresses the substance of the whole picture.

3. Use Cases:

- Picture grouping is utilised in applications, for example,

- Distinguishing objects in photographs (e.g., "Is this picture a feline or a dog?").

- Perceiving manually written digits for digit acknowledgment.

Tensor machine learning

- Content-based picture recovery where you look for pictures because of catchphrases.

4. Frameworks:

- Famous profound learning structures for picture order incorporate TensorFlow, PyTorch, and Keras. Pretrained models like VGG, ResNet, and Commencement are frequently utilized for move learning.

Object Detection:

1. Purpose:

- Object identification goes past picture order by classifying objects in a picture as well as distinguishing their areas. It addresses the inquiry, "What articles are in this image, and where are they found?"

2. Approach:

- Object discovery normally utilises a mix of procedures, frequently founded on CNN models. It incorporates object restriction (bouncing box relapse) and the order of articles inside those jumping boxes.

3. Use Cases:

- Object discovery is utilised in applications, for example,

- Independent driving for distinguishing walkers, vehicles, and traffic signs.

- Observation frameworks for distinguishing interlopers and checking action.

- Expanded reality for putting virtual articles into reality.

- Standardised tag and face recognition in portable applications.

4. Frameworks:

- Famous profound learning structures for object recognition incorporate TensorFlow (utilising the Article Location Programming interface), PyTorch (utilising torchvision), and OpenCV. Models like Quicker R-CNN, Just Go for It (You Just Look Once), and SSD (Single Shot MultiBox Identifier) are generally utilised.

In rundown, picture order is worried about doling out a solitary name to a whole picture, though object recognition distinguishes and confines various items inside a picture. The decision between the two assignments relies upon your particular use case and the degree of detail expected in your application. Object identification is more intricate yet gives more extravagant data about the articles present.

Text classification and sentiment analysis

Message grouping and opinion investigation are normal language handling (NLP) undertakings that include dissecting message information. While they share a few similitudes, they fill various needs:

Text Classification:

1. Purpose:

- Text grouping, otherwise called text arrangement, is the undertaking of doling out predefined classes or names to message reports. It includes putting together and arranging printed information into various classes given their substance.

2. Approach:

- Text grouping normally utilises managed AI procedures and should be possible utilizing different calculations, for example, Credulous Bayes, Backing Vector Machines, or profound learning approaches like repetitive brain organisations (RNNs) and transformers (e.g., BERT).

- The result is the class mark that best addresses the substance or subject of the text report.

3. Use Cases:

- Text characterization is utilised in different applications, including:

- Report arrangement: Putting together news stories into areas like games, legislative issues, and diversion.

- Spam recognition: Recognizing and sifting through spam messages.

- Language ID: Deciding the language of a given text.

- Feeling investigation: Characterizing text because of its tone.

4. Frameworks:

- Text grouping can be executed utilizing NLP libraries and systems like sci-kit-learn, TensorFlow, PyTorch, and Embracing Face Transformers.

Opinion Analysis:

1. Purpose:

- Feeling examination, otherwise called assessment mining, centres around deciding the profound opinion communicated in a piece of text. It is usually used to grasp the extremity (positive, negative, impartial) of the text.

2. Approach:

- Feeling examination should be possible utilising AI, profound learning, or dictionary-based approaches.

- It regularly includes characterising the message into feeling classifications, like good, pessimistic, or impartial, to survey the abstract disposition or assessment communicated in the message.

3. Use Cases:

- Opinion examination is applied in different settings, including:

- Web-based entertainment checking: Examining tweets and presents to grasp public opinion on a theme.

- Item surveys: Deciding client sentiments about an item found on their surveys.

- Client care: Consequently classifying client input as certain or negative.

- Monetary news: Evaluating market feeling because of news stories.

4. Frameworks:

- Opinion examination can be carried out involving similar NLP libraries and systems as message grouping, frequently utilising pre-prepared models custom-fitted for feeling investigation.

In synopsis, message characterization is a more extensive undertaking that sorts messages into predefined classes or classes, while feeling examination is a particular kind of message grouping that spotlights on deciding the close-to-home tone or opinion communicated in a message, like good, pessimistic, or impartial. The two errands assume an essential part in separating important bits of knowledge from literary information in different spaces.

Time series forecasting

Time series estimating is an AI and measurable method used to foresee future qualities in light of verifiable time-requested information. This is a basic errand in different spaces where understanding and foreseeing patterns, examples, and irregularity in information are fundamental. Here is an outline of time series gauging:

Key Ideas in Time Series Forecasting:

1. Time Series Data: Time series information comprises perceptions gathered or recorded at explicit time stretches. It can incorporate authentic stock costs, temperature estimations, marketing projections, and substantially more.

2. Components of Time Series:

- Time series information can frequently be disintegrated into a few parts:

- Trend: The drawn-out development or heading in the information.

- Seasonality: Rehashing examples or varieties at customary stretches.

- Cycle: Non-occasional, rehashing designs, frequently of the longer term.

- Noise: Irregular changes that are not unsurprising.

3. Types of Time Series Forecasting:

- Univariate Forecasting: Foresee a binary variable after some time, which is many times the situation while you're determining a period series given its verifiable information.

- Multivariate Forecasting: Anticipating different factors over the long run, which can be helpful for situations where factors connect or influence one another.

Steps in Time Series Forecasting:

1. Data Collection: Assemble authentic time series information, which might incorporate ordinary periods (e.g., day to day, hourly, month to month).

2. Data Preprocessing:

- Clean the information, handle missing qualities, and manage anomalies.

- Change the information, if necessary, to balance out fluctuations or eliminate patterns.

3. Exploratory Information Investigation (EDA):

- Analyze the information to recognize examples, irregularity, and different attributes.

- Use representation apparatuses to comprehend the time series better.

4. Model Selection:

- Pick a fitting time series determining model given the information's qualities.

- Normal models incorporate autoregressive coordinated moving normal (ARIMA), occasional decay of time series (STL), and further developed models like Prophet, LSTM, or CNNs for time series.

5. Training and Validation:

- Divide the information into preparing and approval sets to prepare and assess the model's presentation.

- Tune hyperparameters, for example, slack requests and irregularity boundaries, for better-gauging results.

6. Model Evaluation:

- Utilise suitable assessment measurements (e.g., Mean Outright Mistake, Mean Squared Blunder, or Root Mean Squared Mistake) to evaluate the model's precision.

7. Forecasting:

- Utilise the prepared model to make expectations for future time spans in light of verifiable information and examples.

8. Visualisation:

- Envision the gauge values alongside certainty stretches to grasp the vulnerability of expectations.

9. Backtesting and Fine-Tuning:

- Ceaselessly assess and refine the model's exhibition with refreshed information.

10. Deployment:

- Convey the time series anticipating model for making ongoing or group expectations.

Time series determining is utilised in different applications, including stock cost expectation, request estimating, energy utilisation expectation, weather conditions gauging, and numerous different fields where verifiable information is basic for pursuing informed future expectations and choices.

Chapter 9: Scaling and Distributed Tensorflow

"Scaling" and "Disseminated TensorFlow" allude to strategies and structures used to work on the presentation and effectiveness of preparing AI models, especially profound learning models. We should investigate the two ideas:

Scaling in TensorFlow:

Scaling in TensorFlow normally includes making the most proficient utilisation of accessible computational assets, like computer processors or GPUs, to speed up preparing and surmising. Here are a few normal strategies for scaling TensorFlow:

1. Data Parallelism:

- Information parallelism includes parting the preparation information into various bunches and dispersing these clumps across various gadgets (e.g., GPUs).

- Every gadget figures slopes on its bunch and offers these inclinations with others, empowering quicker preparation.

2. Model Parallelism:

- Model parallelism is utilised when a model is too huge to even think about squeezing into a solitary gadget's memory.

- The model is divided across different gadgets, and every gadget handles a part of the model.

- Correspondence between these parcels is overseen cautiously.

3. Horovod:

- Horovod is an open-source structure for conveying profound discoveries that can be utilised with TensorFlow.

- It permits you to prepare profound learning models utilising information and model parallelism across numerous GPUs and machines.

4. Distributed Training:

- TensorFlow gives devices like 'tf.distribute.Strategy' for appropriate preparation. You can prepare models across various gadgets and machines, utilising information parallelism and coordinated preparation.

Conveyed TensorFlow:

Conveyed TensorFlow stretches out TensorFlow to work on a disseminated bunch of machines, empowering the preparation of profound learning models at a bigger scope. Key parts of Dispersed TensorFlow include:

1. Parameter Servers:

- Boundary servers are liable for putting away and overseeing model boundaries.

- Labourer undertakings perform calculations utilising these boundaries.

2. Synchronous and Non Concurrent Training:

- Conveyed TensorFlow backings both coordinated (all labourers update simultaneously) and offbeat (labourers update freely) preparing modes.

3. Fault Tolerance:

- Circulated TensorFlow incorporates systems for adaptation to internal failure, guaranteeing that preparation can go on regardless of whether a few machines fizzle.

4. High Performance:

- By circulating calculation, Conveyed TensorFlow completely uses groups of GPUs and central processors, improving the preparation of huge models.

5. TensorFlow Expanded (TFX):

- TFX is a start-to-finish creation prepared stage that incorporates circulated preparation as a feature of its capacities. It permits you to take a model from improvement to organisation at scale.

In common terms, to utilise Conveyed TensorFlow, you want to set up a dispersed processing climate with a bunch of machines and design your TensorFlow code in the same manner. TensorFlow's documentation gives nitty gritty direction on setting up and utilising Conveyed TensorFlow for circulated preparation.

Scaling and appropriating TensorFlow are especially significant for preparing profound learning models on huge datasets, empowering proficient utilisation of assets and quicker model union. They are fundamental for handling complex AI assignments in examination and creation conditions.

Distributed training and tensorflow Extended (TFX)

Conveyed preparation and TensorFlow Expanded (TFX) are two vital parts of the TensorFlow biological system, each filling explicit needs in the AI pipeline.

Circulated Training:

Circulated preparation alludes to the act of preparing AI models across different gadgets, like GPUs or machines, to speed up the preparation cycle. This approach is especially helpful while managing enormous datasets and complex models that require critical computational power. Key parts of conveyed preparation include:

- Information Parallelism: Information parallelism includes parting the preparation of information into various clusters and disseminating these clumps across various gadgets. Every gadget processes angles on its clump and offers these inclinations with others. This approach is valuable for models that fit in memory however requires significant calculation.

- Model Parallelism: Model parallelism is utilised when a model is too huge to even think about squeezing into a solitary gadget's memory. The model is divided across different gadgets, and every gadget handles a piece of the model. Cautious administration of correspondence between allotments is essential.

- Simultaneous and Non Concurrent Training: Appropriated preparing can be coordinated, meaning all specialists update simultaneously, or offbeat, where labourers update autonomously. The decision relies upon factors like synchronisation above and correspondence costs.

- Shortcoming Tolerance: Conveyed preparing structures frequently give systems to adapt to non-critical failure, guaranteeing that preparation can go on regardless of whether a few machines fall flat.

- High Performance: By disseminating calculation, conveyed preparation completely uses groups of GPUs and computer processors, improving the preparation of huge models.

TensorFlow Broadened (TFX):

TensorFlow Broadened (TFX) is a start-to-finish stage for conveying the creation of AI pipelines. It is intended to address the difficulties of taking AI models from improvement to organisation in a versatile, viable, and reproducible way. Key highlights and parts of TFX include:

- ExampleGen: This part ingests information into the pipeline from different sources.

- StatisticsGen: Processes measurements about the information, which helps design and grasp the information's qualities.

- SchemaGen: SchemaGen surmises the pattern of the information, guaranteeing information consistency and quality.

- ExampleValidator: This part recognizes and investigates information abnormalities or issues.

- Transform: Change is utilised for highlighting, designing and preprocessing the information.

- Trainer: The Coach part prepares AI models, frequently involving disseminated preparation methods for huge datasets.

- Tuner and TunerFn (for hyperparameter tuning): TFX gives parts to hyperparameter tuning, which can be urgent for model enhancement.

- InfraValidator: InfraValidator approves that a prepared model can be stacked and served in the creation climate.

- BulkInferrer: This part performs bunch surmising, valuable for running expectations on enormous datasets.

TFX gives an organised and effective method for making, running, and overseeing the AI pipeline's underway conditions. It guarantees information consistency, reproducibility, and adaptability while tending to large numbers of difficulties related with conveying AI models at scale.

In rundown, dispersed preparation speeds up model preparation by circulating calculation across numerous gadgets, while TensorFlow Expanded (TFX) is a start-to-finish stage intended for building and sending creation AI pipelines, guaranteeing vigour, consistency, and versatility in a creation climate.

Tensorflow on GPUs and TPUs

TensorFlow, an open-source AI structure created by Google, offers help for preparing and running AI models on an assortment of equipment gas pedals, including GPUs (Illustrations Handling Units) and TPUs (Tensor Handling Units). We should check out how TensorFlow chips away at these equipment stages:

TensorFlow on GPUs:

1. GPU Acceleration:

- TensorFlow has broad help for running AI responsibilities on GPUs.

- GPUs are especially appropriate for profound learning errands since they can perform numerous framework tasks equally, which are basic to brain network preparation.

2. GPU Compatibility:

- TensorFlow is viable with an extensive variety of GPU models from various makers, including NVIDIA and AMD.

- TensorFlow consequently recognizes and uses accessible GPUs, and you can indicate which GPUs to utilise assuming you have different gadgets.

3. GPU-Explicit Operations:

- TensorFlow permits you to assign explicit activities to run on GPUs, including model preparation and deduction, profiting from GPU speed increase.

4. GPU Memory Management:

- TensorFlow oversees GPU memory, including dispensing and deallocating memory depending on the situation during preparation. It can likewise stay away from out-of-memory mistakes with methods like memory fracture.

5. CuDNN Integration:

- TensorFlow coordinates with the NVIDIA cuDNN library, which is profoundly advanced for profound learning jobs, further improving GPU execution.

TensorFlow on TPUs:

1. TPU Acceleration:

- TPUs, or Tensor Handling Units, are specially crafted equipment gas pedals by Google for AI responsibilities, particularly custom-made for TensorFlow.

- TPUs offer noteworthy execution and are accessible on Google Cloud.

2. Cloud TPU Support:

- TensorFlow can be utilised with Cloud TPUs on Google Cloud Stage, giving admittance to these strong gas pedals for model preparation and derivation.

3. TPU-Explicit Operations:

- TensorFlow has TPU-explicit tasks that can be utilised to proficiently run calculations on TPUs.

4. TPU Distribution:

- Conveyed preparation with TPUs is upheld, empowering the equal preparation of enormous models across different TPUs.

5. Tensor Handling Unit Cases (TPU Pods):

- Google offers TPU Cases, which are assortments of TPUs interconnected to give considerably real figuring power. TensorFlow backs these TPU Cases for very elite execution preparation.

The decision among GPUs and TPUs relies upon your particular necessities, spending plan, and accessibility. GPUs are generally accessible and support different jobs. TPUs, then again, offer predominant execution however are accessible on Google Cloud.

Tensor machine learning

TensorFlow's adaptability permits you to foster your models on a computer processor and afterward exploit GPU or TPU speed increase for more productive preparation. It's critical to choose the fitting equipment assets given the size of your information, model intricacy, and accessible financial plan.

Chapter 10: Case studies

Contextual analyses are to bottom assessments of explicit certifiable circumstances or undertakings, frequently utilised in different fields, including business, medical care, designing, and information science, to break down and gain from common sense encounters. Here are a few instances of contextual investigations in various spaces:

Business and Marketing:

1. Coca-Cola's Substance 2020 Initiative:

- An examination of Coca-Cola's fruitful substance showcasing technique, zeroing in on their "Content 2020" drive, which is expected to twofold deals while decreasing publicising costs.

2. Amazon's Client Driven Approach:

- A contextual investigation investigating how Amazon's tireless spotlight on client experience has prompted its predominance in the web-based business industry.

Medical services and Medicine:

1. Johns Hopkins Emergency Clinic's Patient Wellbeing Program:

- An assessment of how Johns Hopkins Emergency Clinic carried out a patient well-being program, bringing about a huge decrease in clinical mistakes.

2. The Battle Against Coronavirus 19:

- Numerous contextual investigations on different nations' reactions to the Coronavirus pandemic, examining their techniques and results.

Designing and Technology:

1. SpaceX's Reusable Rockets:

- A contextual investigation of SpaceX's accomplishment in creating and reusing rocket innovation, prompting a change in perspective in the space business.

2. Tesla's Electric Vehicles:

- An examination of Tesla's electric vehicle assembling, dispersion, and maintainable energy drives.

Information Science and Machine Learning:

1. Netflix's Proposal System:

- A contextual investigation of how Netflix utilises AI calculations to prescribe customised content to its clients.

2. DeepMind's AlphaGo:

- An examination of DeepMind's AlphaGo project, which exhibited the force of profound support learning in dominating the complicated prepackaged game Go.

Ecological and Sustainability:

1. The Curitiba Transport Fast Travel System:

- A contextual investigation of Curitiba, Brazil's imaginative public transportation framework, which has turned into a model for maintainable metropolitan preparation.

2. Renewable Energy Progress in Germany:

- An assessment of Germany's "Energiewende" (energy progress) strategy, which expects to move to sustainable power sources and lessen fossil fuel byproducts.

Training and Learning:

1. Khan Institute's Customised Learning:

- A contextual investigation of Khan Institute's internet-based instructive stage and its way of dealing with customised growth opportunities.

2. Finland's Schooling System:

- An investigation of Finland's school system, known for its imaginative showing techniques and reliably high understudy execution.

Contextual analyses are significant for gaining from both examples of overcoming adversity and difficulties looked at in certifiable applications They give bits of knowledge into independent direction, critical thinking, and the effect of different systems and innovations. While leading or looking into contextual analyses, it's fundamental to think about the specific situation, targets, and results to make significant inferences and apply illustrations to figure out how to future undertakings.

Real-world machine learning projects

Certifiable AI projects range in different spaces and applications, displaying the viable utilisation of AI strategies to take care of complicated issues. Here are instances of certifiable AI projects:

1.Fraud Recognition in Monetary Transactions:

- Monetary organisations use AI to recognize deceitful charge card exchanges, safeguard clients, and limit monetary misfortunes.

2. Recommendation Systems:

- Organisations like Netflix, Amazon, and Spotify influence proposal calculations to recommend content or items to clients given their inclinations and ways of behaving.

3. Medical Picture Analysis:

- AI is utilised to examine clinical pictures like X-beams, X-rays, and CT outputs to help radiologists in illness discovery and finding.

4. Natural Language Handling for Client Support:

- Organisations utilise chatbots and opinion investigation to further develop client assistance via mechanising reactions, understanding client questions, and checking client fulfilment.

5. Predictive Support in Manufacturing:

- Makers use AI to anticipate gear disappointments and timetable upkeep, lessening free time and support costs.

6. Autonomous Vehicles:

- Organisations like Waymo and Tesla utilise AI models for independent driving, including object recognition, path following, and dynamic calculations.

7. Social Media Opinion Analysis:

- Virtual entertainment stages use feeling investigation to comprehend client assessments and patterns, assisting organisations with pursuing informed choices and answering client input.

8. Crop Yield Expectation in Agriculture:

- AI models are used to conjecture crop yields because of climate information, assisting ranchers with settling on better conclusions about planting and reaping.

9. Energy Utilisation Forecasting:

- Energy organisations use AI to foresee energy interest, advance asset distribution, and improve energy effectiveness.

10. Speech Acknowledgment and Virtual Assistants:

- Voice-actuated menial helpers like Siri and Alexa use discourse acknowledgment models to comprehend and answer voice orders.

11. A/B Testing and Change Rate Optimization:

- Online business and online stages utilise A/B testing and AI to improve site page designs, item suggestions, and promotion situations to increment change rates.

12. Recommendation of Medical services Treatments:

- AI assists medical services experts with making customized therapy suggestions because of patient information and clinical history.

13. Language Translation:

- Administrations like Google Interpret use brain-machine interpretation models to give interpretations across various dialects.

14. Credit Scoring and Hazard Assessment:

- Banks and loaning foundations utilise AI models to evaluate the reliability of credit candidates and ascertain loaning risk.

15. E-trade Request Forecasting:

- Retailers use AI to foresee item interest, oversee stock, and enhance production network activities.

16. Environment and Environment Modeling:

- Environment researchers use AI to dissect authentic environment information and make expectations about future environment examples and patterns.

These genuine ventures feature the adaptability and effect of AI across assorted areas. They address basic difficulties, upgrade direction, computerised errands, and further develop client encounters, showing the critical job of AI in this day and age.

Ethical considerations in machine learning

Moral contemplations in AI are of central significance, as AI models and calculations can influence people, society, and different parts of life. Tending to these moral worries is pivotal for capable computer-based intelligence improvement. Here are a few vital moral contemplations in AI:

1. Fairness and Bias:

- Guaranteeing that AI models are fair and unprejudiced is a major moral concern. Inclination can prompt segregation and uncalled-for treatment of specific gatherings. Engineers ought to effectively moderate inclination and guarantee models treat all people similarly.

2. Privacy:

- AI frequently includes the utilisation of individual information. It's fundamental to safeguard client protection by carrying out hearty information security and safety efforts, anonymizing information, and complying with security guidelines like GDPR and CCPA.

3. Transparency and Explainability:

- The "discovery" nature of some AI models can make it trying to comprehend how they show up at choices. Engineers ought to endeavour to make models more interpretable and give clarifications to their forecasts.

4. Accountability and Responsibility:

- Laying out clear lines of liability regarding simulated intelligence and AI frameworks is fundamental. Engineers and associations ought to be responsible for the effect of their frameworks on society.

5. Data Assortment and Informed Consent:

- Moral information assortment rehearses incorporate getting educated assent, guaranteeing information is utilised exclusively for planned purposes, and permitting people to control their information.

6. Use Cases and Application:

- Thought ought to be given to the possible mischief and abuse of AI in applications like observation, independent weapons, and different areas where the innovation might hurt.

7. Discrimination Mitigation:

- Engineers ought to effectively attempt to moderate and address segregation in AI frameworks, especially when it concerns delicate qualities like race, orientation, and handicap.

8. Algorithmic Governance:

- Moral rules and administration designs ought to be set up to administer and direct AI frameworks, guaranteeing consistency with moral norms.

9. Bias Testing and Auditing:

- Customary testing and reviewing of AI models for predisposition is important to recognize and redress likely issues.

10. Accessibility:

- Guaranteeing that AI advancements are open to all, incorporating people with disabilities, is fundamental for the comprehensive turn of events.

11. Social and Natural Impact:

- Designers ought to consider the more extensive effect of AI on society, including its natural impression and its ramifications for business and disparity.

12. Education and Literacy:

- Advancing man-made intelligence and AI proficiency among the general population and chiefs is essential to cultivating informed conversations and choices about artificial intelligence morals.

13. Ethics Audit Boards:

- Laying out morals audit sheets can assist associations with assessing the moral ramifications of their AI tasks and choices.

14. Global Perspectives:

- Perceive that computer-based intelligence morals is a worldwide issue, and think about social and provincial contrasts in moral standards and values.

Tending to these moral contemplations includes interdisciplinary cooperation, straightforwardness, and progressing exchange among computer-based intelligence specialists, ethicists, policymakers, and the general population. Moral artificial intelligence advancement guarantees that AI innovations are utilised to support mankind while regarding individual freedoms and values.

Future trends in tensorflow and machine learning

The field of AI and TensorFlow is ceaselessly developing, with a few outstanding patterns and headings forming its future. Here are a few critical future patterns in TensorFlow and AI:

1. Efficiency and Scalability:

- Future variants of TensorFlow are probably going to zero in on further enhancing model preparation and derivation for different equipment stages, including GPUs, TPUs, and edge gadgets.

2. AutoML and Robotized Machine Learning:

- The improvement of AutoML apparatuses that computerise parts of the AI pipeline, from information preprocessing to demonstrating determination and hyperparameter tuning, will keep on developing.

3. Interoperability and Biological System Growth:

- TensorFlow will upgrade its similarity with other AI structures and advance interoperability. It will additionally foster a biological system of libraries and instruments for different AI undertakings.

4. Explainable artificial intelligence and Model Interpretability:

- The interest in interpretable AI models will rise, and TensorFlow is probably going to coordinate more apparatuses for model logic to meet these necessities.

5. Federated Learning:

- TensorFlow will keep on creating unified learning abilities, permitting AI models to be prepared across decentralised information sources while safeguarding protection.

6. Quantum Machine Learning:

- TensorFlow will investigate quantum AI, utilising quantum figuring for complex critical thinking and streamlining assignments.

7. Natural Language Handling (NLP) Advancements:

- TensorFlow will add to the progression of NLP with further developed models, pre-prepared language portrayals, and multilingual abilities.

8. Self-Regulated Learning:

- Self-regulated realisation, where models gain from unlabeled information, will acquire unmistakable quality, prompting work on model speculation.

9. Robotics and Support Learning:

- TensorFlow will keep on being at the front of advanced mechanics and support picking up, making it simpler to prepare robots for complex true errands.

10. Responsible simulated intelligence and Ethics:

- Moral simulated intelligence advancement will be underlined with apparatuses for inclination moderation, reasonableness, and model logic coordinated into TensorFlow.

11. Edge man-made intelligence and IoT Integration:

- TensorFlow will additionally uphold running AI models of anxious gadgets, working with the sending of simulated intelligence on IoT gadgets for continuous handling.

12. Quantum Machine Learning:

- Innovative work in quantum AI will keep on investigating the capability of quantum figuring in tackling complex issues.

13. Lifelong Learning:

- Procedures for nonstop realisation, where models can adjust to new information after some time, will turn out to be more vital in different applications.

14. Advanced PC Vision:

- TensorFlow will keep on propelling PC vision abilities, with more exact and proficient item identification and picture acknowledgment models.

15. Explainable artificial intelligence and Model Interpretability:

- Expanding emphasis on getting it and deciphering the choices made by AI models, particularly in applications like medical services and money.

16. Multi-Modular Learning:

- Joining various information modalities, like text, pictures, and sound, to make all the more remarkable and set mindful models.

These patterns mirror the developing scene of AI, driven by both mechanical headways and cultural requests. TensorFlow, as one of the main AI structures, will assume a vital part in these turns of events, adding to the development and advancement in the field. Designers and specialists ought to remain refreshed on these patterns to use the maximum capacity of TensorFlow and AI later on.

Conclusion

In the determination of the book on Tensor Machine Learning, Jeffery M. Falgoust commonly sums up the vital points and features of the excursion from the essentials to cutting-edge applications. It could address the accompanying focuses:

1. Recap of Fundamentals: A concise survey of the key ideas shrouded in the book, for example, information preprocessing, model engineering, and improvement procedures.

2. Progression of Knowledge: The writer might underscore how perusers have advanced beginner students to have a more profound comprehension of AI standards and TensorFlow.

3. Advanced Application: The end frequently examines the further developed applications that were investigated in the book, showing the common sense of AI in true situations.

4. Ethical Considerations: A notice of the significance of moral contemplations in AI, including reasonableness, straightforwardness, and protection, and how they tended to throughout the book.

5. Future Directions: The creator could offer experiences into the future of TensorFlow and AI, talking about arising patterns and the expected effect of the innovation.

6. Acknowledgment and Encouragement: A note of appreciation to the perusers for their excursion through the book and consolation to keep investigating and applying AI ideas.

7. Resources and Further Learning: The end might give extra assets to perusers to proceed with their learning process, including references to online courses, research papers, and TensorFlow documentation.

The decision ordinarily fills in as a reflection on the information acquired, a source of inspiration for additional investigation, and a sign of the significance of moral and mindful utilisation of AI advancements. It leaves perusers with a feeling of achievement and inspiration to proceed with their AI tries.